The Pre-Writing Handbook
for Law Students

The Pre-Writing Handbook for Law Students

A Step-by-Step Guide

Second Edition

Laura P. Graham
Miriam E. Felsenburg

CAROLINA ACADEMIC PRESS

Durham, North Carolina

Library of Congress Cataloging-in-Publication Data

Names: Graham, Laura P., author. | Felsenburg, Miriam E., author.
Title: The pre-writing handbook for law students : a step-by-step guide / by
    Laura P. Graham, Miriam E. Felsenburg.
Description: Second edition. | Durham, North Carolina : Carolina Academic
    Press, LLC, [2019] | Includes bibliographical references and index.
Identifiers: LCCN 2019016402 | ISBN 9781531013226 (alk. paper)
Subjects: LCSH: Legal composition.
Classification: LCC KF250 .G725 2019 | DDC 808.06/634--dc23
LC record available at https://lccn.loc.gov/2019016402

e-ISBN 978-1-5310-1323-3

Carolina Academic Press
700 Kent Street
Durham, North Carolina 27701
Telephone (919) 489-7486
Fax (919) 493-5668
www.cap-press.com

Printed in the United States of America

I dedicate this book to Deborah Leonard Parker and Christine Nero Coughlin, two amazing legal writing directors who have made my job a joy; and to Joseph and Ellen, who make the rest of my life a joy.

Laura P. Graham

This book is dedicated to the memory of my beloved Mother, Gertrud K. Felsenburg, Ph.D., who would be very proud; and to Regina.

Miriam E. Felsenburg

Contents

Acknowledgments

First and foremost, I would like to acknowledge my friend and former colleague, Miriam E. (Miki) Felsenburg, my co-author on the first edition of *The Pre-Writing Handbook*. Miki is now enjoying her well-deserved retirement, and I am grateful that she trusted me to revise the first edition on my own. This book is really Miki's in many ways; she first envisioned it more than ten years ago, and she kept our work on track until the first edition was released in 2013. This new edition bears her fingerprint on each page.

Second, I would like to thank my Legal Analysis, Writing, and Research colleagues here at Wake Forest University School of Law, who always provide encouragement and thoughtful feedback on every project I undertake. I am particularly indebted to Christine Coughlin, Elizabeth Johnson, Russell Gold, John Korzen, and Heather Gram, who generously allowed me to use their work product as the basis for the new Independent Practice Exercises in this edition.

Third, I would like to thank Dean Suzanne Reynolds, Executive Associate Dean for Academic Affairs Jonathan Cardi, and Associate Dean for Research, Public Engagement, and Faculty Development Gregory Parks, whose commitment to support the scholar-teacher model makes it possible for my Wake Forest colleagues and me to undertake projects like this book revision. I am also grateful to Cynthia Ring, administrative professional extraordinaire, who somehow always seems to know what I need before I need it.

Fourth, I would like to thank my legal writing colleagues across the country, especially those who have used the first edition of *The Pre-Writing Handbook* with their students and have shared valuable insights about how the book could be improved. I hope this new edition is responsive to their suggestions.

Finally, I would like to thank the many students at Wake Forest University School of Law who have diligently worked through the first edition of *The Pre-Writing Handbook*. They have sharpened my own understanding of the role pre-writing plays in the work of novice legal writers. And through their struggles and eventual successes, they have confirmed my conviction that time spent focusing on pre-writing, early and often, pays great dividends throughout their law school years and beyond.

Laura P. Graham
May 2019

Introduction

Effective legal writers are, by definition, effective legal analysts. Almost every form of legal writing involves communicating legal analysis. And like learning any other skill, learning to be an effective legal analyst and writer requires practice and patience.

The Pre-Writing Handbook for Law Students is designed to help you develop and practice the skills that will allow you to effectively analyze legal questions to arrive at sound answers about which you are confident. The confidence you gain from engaging in the *pre-writing process* outlined in the *Handbook* will then translate into a smoother, more effective *writing process* and a better written product.

While we hope that the *Handbook* will be useful to legal writers in many contexts beyond the first-year classroom, we have deliberately geared it toward beginning legal writers, who often find the going tough. We have confirmed through careful research that many beginning legal writers struggle in part because they underestimate the key role that legal analysis plays in effective legal writing; they believe that effective legal writing is primarily a matter of style and format. Of course, those aspects of legal writing are important to the finished *product*—the memo or brief that will ultimately be submitted to the supervising attorney or to the court. But long before style and format come into play, the legal writer must engage in the *process* of deciding what the document should say. We refer to this process as the *pre-writing process*.

Routinely engaging in the pre-writing process is especially important for novice legal writers, because legal analysis is more complex, and often more difficult, than they expect. Legal analysis demands a level of independent critical thinking that does not come naturally to many beginning law students. The law is often ambiguous, and conclusions are often difficult to come by. And how you arrive at your answer to a legal question is just as important to your eventual legal reader as the answer itself. Legal analysts must train themselves to keep their minds open from the moment they begin thinking about a legal question until the moment they are certain they have every piece of available information needed to answer that question.

Moreover, effective legal analysis rests in part on a conscious engagement in metacognitive processes. Metacognition has been defined as "thinking about thinking." As you analyze a legal question, you need to pause periodically to evaluate your progress. You need to train yourself to recognize gaps in your understanding and to address them before moving forward. Most beginning law students are already good metacognitive learners; the pre-writing strategies in the *Handbook* are designed to help you become even more deliberate about using metacognitive strategies to enhance your analytical skills.

Throughout the *Handbook*, we have identified crucial metacognitive "checkpoints" in the pre-writing process—points where you should slow down, or perhaps stop, to assess your progress and to make any necessary adjustments. Each checkpoint is labeled with either a "pause" symbol ❿ or a "stop" symbol ⭘. We urge you not to skip these important checkpoints, because they identify key opportunities to become more adept at monitoring and refining your pre-writing process.

We have deliberately limited the scope of the *Handbook*. While it addresses all of the steps in the *pre-writing process*, it does not discuss all of those steps in equal depth. For example, while Chapter 5 discusses the role of legal research in the pre-writing process, it does not detail the many and varied methods of conducting legal research; we proceed on the assumption that you will receive comprehensive legal research instruction as part of your first-year curriculum. On the other hand, the *Handbook* spends a great deal of time on the pre-writing steps that should happen *after* the legal research is done.

The *Handbook* only briefly introduces the steps in the *writing process*—that is, the steps involved in producing a finished written product, such as a memo or brief. We consider outlining, drafting, editing, revising, polishing, citing, etc. to be beyond the scope of the *pre-writing process*. The *Handbook* proceeds on the assumption that you will receive comprehensive legal writing instruction as part of your first-year curriculum.

That is not to say that there is no writing involved in pre-writing. At each step of the pre-writing process, you will be encouraged to put the results of your work in writing. However, your written record of your pre-writing work is intended for one audience only—you. Thus, there is great flexibility in terms of what it looks like. We have suggested some formats for recording your pre-writing work, but these formats are not "magic"—you should feel free to adapt them to suit your purposes, or even to create your own formats. The key is to discipline yourself to capture your work at each step of the pre-writing process in a written form that you can return to at later points in your process. In the recap at the end of each chapter, we provide a running list of the written products that should be generated during the pre-writing process.

The Pre-Writing Handbook for Law Students offers specific techniques for making pre-writing a regular part of your process when working on legal writing assignments. These techniques are illustrated in the context of a typical first-year legal writing assignment, in which the junior attorney (the student) receives information about a case from a senior attorney or supervisor (the professor) and is asked to produce a specific legal document (a memo, a trial brief, etc.). Of course, this is but one of many contexts in which legal analysis is required, but it is a context that will be immediately familiar to most users of the *Handbook.*

Each chapter of the *Handbook* contains detailed illustrations of the steps in the pre-writing process, using two well-developed scenarios from different areas of the law. Each chapter also includes exercises based on four additional scenarios, so that you can independently practice the pre-writing skills explained in that chapter. We urge you to complete all of the exercises in each chapter, even if your professor does not require you to; the exercises build on one another, and each individual exercise will benefit you more if you have completed the prior exercises.

As these scenarios are developed throughout the *Handbook*, you will notice that heavy emphasis is placed on the crucial skill of recognizing the narrow legal issues that must be analyzed in order to answer the broad questions the scenarios present. To assist you in developing that skill, we have included in the recap at the end of every chapter a description of the issues in the two scenarios, as refined by your work in that step of the pre-writing process.

Precisely because the *Handbook* emphasizes the need to move slowly and deliberately through the pre-writing process, we urge you to move slowly and deliberately through the *Handbook* itself. More than likely, your professor will break your reading of the *Handbook* into many small chunks, and this is a good thing. As you will see in Chapter 6, close, active reading is a vital skill for both beginning law students and seasoned lawyers; thus, close, active reading of the *Handbook* itself is required in order for you to get the maximum value out of it.

Chapter 1 provides an overview of the four stages of the pre-writing process; Chapters 2 through 8 elaborate on the individual steps within those four stages; and Chapter 9 briefly discusses the transition from the pre-writing process to the writing process. We believe that by reading the *Handbook* and completing the exercises, you will gain a level of confidence in your legal analysis skills that will propel you towards becoming an excellent legal writer.

The Pre-Writing Handbook for Law Students

Chapter 1

An Overview of the Four Stages of the Pre-Writing Process

At a basic level, the work of a lawyer almost always requires analyzing legal questions. Competent lawyers are able to analyze legal questions in virtually any area of the law, and they usually conduct their analyses in a predictable way. In fact, the process of legal analysis is predictable enough that its various components can be outlined and learned, step by step. We call this step-by-step process the *pre-writing process*.

In the *Handbook*, the pre-writing process is broken down into four stages:

- Getting your bearings;
- Locating and reading the relevant authorities;
- Building a bridge between reading and analysis; and
- Analyzing your narrow issues.

Each of these four stages is further broken down into smaller steps, as follows:

- Getting your bearings
  - Understanding the story
  - Understanding your specific assignment

- Locating and reading the relevant authorities
  - Formulating a research plan
  - Incorporating research into your pre-writing process
  - Reading and assessing the relevant authorities

- Building a bridge between reading and analysis
  - Identifying analogical categories
  - Creating a visual representation of your analogical categories

- Analyzing your narrow issues
  - Analysis using rule-based reasoning
  - Analysis using analogical reasoning
  - Counteranalysis

1.1 Getting Your Bearings

The first stage of the pre-writing process, *getting your bearings*, consists of two steps: *understanding the story* and *understanding your specific assignment.* Every legal analysis begins with a story, and a good legal analyst seeks to understand that story to the greatest extent possible before moving forward. Thus, at the outset of any legal writing assignment, you should take the time to begin to distill the aspects of the story that really matter. You should not yet be making definitive judgments about the significance of particular facts; your goals here are to identify the broad legal questions raised by the story and to *preliminarily* identify the facts that may be important in answering those questions. As part of this step, you should make some notes about your initial understanding of the story. Charts, bulleted lists of key facts, timelines, and retelling are some useful techniques for note-taking; some of these techniques are illustrated in Chapter 2.

Once you understand the story, the next step is to understand your assignment. Every legal writing assignment falls within certain broad parameters, and a good legal analyst seeks to understand what those parameters are before moving forward. Thus, at the outset of any legal writing assignment, you should ask yourself certain questions: Where am I in the life of this problem? What exactly has my supervising attorney asked me to do? How long do I have to do it? The answers to these and other similar questions will furnish the context for your analytical work and will help you plan your research. Chapter 3 provides specific strategies for understanding your assignment and recording your understanding in a useful written form.

1.2 Locating and Reading the Relevant Authorities

The second stage of the pre-writing process, *locating and reading the relevant authorities,* consists of three steps: *formulating a research plan, incorporating research into your pre-writing process,* and *reading and assessing the relevant authorities.*

Once you understand both the story and your specific assignment, you are ready to search for the authorities that will help you refine (and ultimately answer) the broad legal questions you preliminarily identified in your earlier pre-writing. This is where legal research enters the pre-writing process. You should think of research not as separate from the pre-writing process, but as an integral part of it.

Before you dive into your research, you need to formulate a good research plan. To do this, you need to spend some time brainstorming about what you hope to learn from your research. You may also need to spend some time educating yourself about the subjects of your broad legal questions, so that you can read the authorities with a clearer focus. This brainstorming should result in a written list of possible narrower issues for exploration. Then, after considering any aspects of your as-signment that may impact your research plan—jurisdictional limitations or references to particular authorities in your supervising attorney's assigning memo, for example—you are ready to write down a tentative research plan. Chapter 4 explains how to develop a research plan and suggests a useful template for writing down that plan.

The next step in your pre-writing process is executing your research plan. The *Handbook* does not attempt to teach you the specifics of how to research. Rather, it suggests strategies for effectively incorporating research into your pre-writing process. Chapter 5 discusses some helpful methods for making a careful written record of your research. It also suggests strategies for organizing the authorities you find, so that your reading of those authorities will be more efficient and so that you can spot any gaps in your research.

When you are satisfied that your research has led you to most, if not all, of the authorities that will help you further refine and later answer your broad legal questions, you can move to the final step of this stage: reading and assessing the relevant authorities. Chapter 6 outlines a strategy for accomplishing this step. This strategy is illustrated using two different hypothetical scenarios involving a wide variety of authorities. Close, active reading of the authorities is one of the most important steps in the entire pre-writing process, and you should not move forward in your work until you have arrived at a thorough un-derstanding of the rules and reasoning of each relevant authority.

1.3 Building a Bridge Between Reading and Analysis

The third stage of the pre-writing process, *building a bridge between reading and analysis,* involves two steps: *identifying the analogical categories* that were central to the results in the relevant authorities and then *creating a visual representation* of the results of your categorization. In some scenarios, categorizing the facts will be fairly straightforward; in others, it will be quite complex. Correct identification of the relevant categories is critical for two reasons. First, it allows you to refine your issues even further, so that you know exactly what narrow issues you must analyze in order to answer the broad questions you identified in your early pre-writing work. Second, it paves the way for you to efficiently and correctly analyze those narrow issues when you reach that stage of the pre-writing process. Chapter 7 introduces you to analogical reasoning and walks you through the process of identifying the relevant categories of fact within the authorities so that you can use analogical reasoning to resolve your narrow issues.

The second step in the bridge-building stage is to create a visual representation of the results of your categorization. In this step, you have the freedom to construct your visual in any way that usefully captures your categorization; Chapter 7 provides two examples of useful visuals. Your visual will be a vital tool as you complete your pre-writing process.

1.4 Analyzing Your Narrow Issues

The final stage of the pre-writing process is *analyzing your narrow issues.* If you have done a thorough job at each of the three previous stages, your analysis should proceed fairly smoothly, even if your narrow issues are complex. Chapter 8 elaborates on the two most common kinds of legal reasoning that lawyers use to analyze legal questions—*rule-based reasoning* and *analogical reasoning.* It then illustrates each kind of reasoning using the same two scenarios as in the previous chapters. It also discusses the role and importance of *counteranalysis.* When you have completed your analysis, you will be able to confidently predict the most likely resolution of the narrow issues upon which the answers to the broad questions turn.

Legal analysis is not a science, and the law is sometimes inherently ambiguous. As a new law student, you may sometimes feel frustrated when your analysis does not produce definitive answers to your legal questions. It is important for you to realize that, often, the best you can do is to give your supervising attorney the "more likely" or "better" answers. In such circumstances, your thorough work during the pre-writing process will enable you to have confidence in your answers and will allow you to enter the writing process with a deeper understanding of the analysis you must communicate in your written product.

Chapter 2

Understanding the Story

Suppose you decide to take a trip from your hometown of Denver to Vancouver, B.C.—a city you've never visited before. You decide to travel by car, so that you can take in the scenery along the way. If you had all the time in the world, you could simply get in your car and head north and west, hoping that you would make it to Vancouver eventually. But if that were all the "planning" you did, your journey would be long and difficult, you would be lost much of the time, and you might never get to Vancouver.

A better approach would be to spend some time in advance "getting your bearings" as to the journey ahead. You could hop on the internet and find maps showing the possible routes from Denver to Vancouver, information on good places to stop along the way, estimates of the mileage and travel time, etc. You could also research Vancouver itself, so that you would have a preliminary idea of what you would like to do when you get there.

Tackling a legal analysis without first getting your bearings is like traveling from Denver to Vancouver without any advance planning. Your work will be difficult, it will be inefficient, you will probably get lost along the way, and you might never find a good answer to your legal question. The pre-writing process is the map that will guide your journey from the initial question to the final answer, and the first stage in that process is *getting your bearings*—that is, spending adequate time familiarizing yourself with the story that gives rise to the questions you've been asked to answer and the specific assignment you've been asked to complete.

Assume you have received the following e-mail from your supervising attorney:

Figure 2-1   Assigning E-mail from Supervising Attorney

MEMORANDUM

To: Junior Associate
From: Paula Cox, Senior Partner
Re: Client Arthur Byrd
            Alleged violation of Graburg red-light statute
Date: July 15, 2019

Our client, Arthur Byrd, was ticketed by Officer Jan Sprouse on the public roadway at the intersection of Main Street and Cemetery Road in downtown Salem. Mr. Byrd had just crossed the intersection on a Segway i2 SE. The light in his direction of travel was red. He was using the Segway because he had a sprained ankle and was unable to walk extended distances. He borrowed his neighbor's Segway to run a quick errand to the drugstore.

Mr. Byrd was ticketed for violating the State of Graburg's red-light statute. My recollection is that the language of the red-light statute only applies to someone driving "a vehicle such as an automobile." Please write a memo to the file assessing whether this charge can stick. ❶ I think the case is calendared for early September, and I need to decide how to advise Mr. Byrd.

> ❶ Note that informal language is common in e-mails, but you should not parrot it in your final product.

What is the first step you should take?

Intuitively, you would begin by reading quickly though the e-mail. This quick reading reveals (a) that, at a basic level, the problem involves a man who ran a red light while riding a Segway i2 SE,[1] and (b) that Attorney Cox needs to know whether this violated the Graburg red-light statute.

You might be tempted at this point to assume an answer: "Of course a Segway rider has to obey the red-light statute" or "That's just a ridiculous charge." This would be a mistake for several reasons.

First, the question Attorney Cox posed is a very broad one: Can the charge "stick"? Put another way, is Mr. Byrd likely to be convicted under the red-light statute? At this point, you have no idea what *specific* narrow issues must be resolved in order to predict the answer to the broad question of whether the charge can stick. Second, you have only limited knowledge of the facts, and you have no way of knowing what facts will matter in deciding whether the charge can stick.

---

1. This is the basic model of personal Segway available at the time of this writing.

Even this simple scenario requires you to develop a deeper under-standing of the "story" before your work can progress efficiently. To get this deeper understanding, you will need to reread your assignment, paying attention to every detail. Your goal here is not to filter or weed out any facts; you don't yet know enough about the law to allow you to label any fact as "important" or "not important." Your goals are to flesh out the story as much as possible based on what you know so far and to identify any obvious gaps in the facts.

A simple way to record your deeper understanding of the story is to make a bulleted list of the aspects of the story that seem important. For the Segway scenario, your list might look something like the list in Figure 2-2:

Figure 2-2 Preliminary List of Important Facts in Segway Scenario

- Mr. Byrd was riding a borrowed Segway.
- He was on a specific errand (not recreational riding).
- He was riding the Segway because he had a sprained ankle.
- He was riding directly on the street (not on a sidewalk, a driveway, inside a building, etc.).
- He was downtown (greater likelihood of vehicle/pedestrian traffic).
- He went through a red light.
- He's been charged with violating the Graburg red-light statute, which applies to "a vehicle such as an automobile." ⬤

> ⬤ This list includes some information that results from "reading between the lines." The e-mail doesn't say that there was a lot of vehicular or pedestrian traffic, but the fact that the incident occurred downtown (as opposed to on a rural road) permits the inference that there was at least some vehicular and/or pedestrian traffic nearby. Don't be afraid to draw reasonable inferences, although you should always verify their accuracy.

The list of facts in Figure 2-2 seems fairly straightforward, and it summarizes Mr. Byrd's story pretty well. But if you study the list carefully, you will realize that it does much more than just *summarize facts*; it *points you toward the narrower issue* that this situation raises. Just by looking at the first and last items on the list, you can see that the charge against Mr. Byrd will stick (the broad question) only if the Segway is "a vehicle such as an automobile" (the narrower issue).

Moreover, once you understand that you're going to have to figure out whether a Segway is "a vehicle such as an automobile," you can spot a likely gap in your factual knowledge. Unless you own a Segway, or have had extensive experience riding one, you will need to find out more about the Segway, so you can compare it to an automobile. It is perfectly fine to include in your summary of the story any follow-up questions you need to investigate. Thus, you might add another bullet to your list:

  • Find out more about the Segway i2 SE.

At this point, you may think that the narrow issue—whether the Segway is "a vehicle such an automobile"—has an easy answer. Rest assured that it does not. In each subsequent chapter of the *Handbook*, your appreciation of its complexity will grow; but you will also learn how to manage the process of arriving at an answer to a complex question by breaking down the process into several concrete steps.

A bulleted list of the important aspects of the story will serve you well no matter what the scenario involves. In fact, the more complex the scenario, the more useful your bulleted list will be, because there is more to understand and remember. For example, suppose you have received the following e-mail:

Figure 2-3   Assigning E-mail from Supervising Attorney

To: Junior Associate
From: Paula Cox, Senior Partner
Sent: October 15, 2018
Subject: Alice Ward's possible breach of warranty claim

This morning I met with a potential client, Ms. Alice Ward. Ms. Ward is a resident of South Carolina who purchased a new Laundrolux washing machine at Major Appliances, Inc. on September 30, 2015. The machine came with a one-year manufacturer's warranty, and Ms. Ward purchased an additional two-year extended warranty on the machine through Major Appliances, Inc. When the machine broke in July 2018, Ms. Ward was too busy to deal with it right away. She finally got around to contacting Laundrolux, who told her to contact Major Appliances, Inc. because the one-year Laundrolux manufacturer's warranty had expired.

On September 27, 2018, Ms. Ward found the extended warranty and the accompanying claim form in her files. She completed the form and put it in an envelope with proper postage addressed to Major Appliances, Inc. at the address listed on the form. Later that day, she took the envelope to her local Ace Hardware store, which maintains a post office annex. She handed the envelope to the clerk, Maria Jones, who frequently handles Ms. Ward's mail.

Eleven days later, on October 8, 2018, Ms. Ward realized that she had not received a response from Major Appliances, Inc., and she called the local store. When she was finally connected to someone in the warranty department, she was told that Major Appliances, Inc. had never received her claim and that the warranty had expired on September 30, 2018. Ms.

Ward cannot afford to buy a new washing machine, and she would like to know whether we can help her enforce the warranty.

I think that this transaction may fall under the common law "mailbox rule." If it does, we may be able to help Ms. Ward. Please look into this matter and draft a letter to Ms. Ward advising her of her options. Ms. Ward has been calling me daily to inquire about the matter, so please get this letter drafted right away.

As with the Segway scenario, you should begin your pre-writing process by making a bulleted list of the aspects of Ms. Ward's story that seem important. That list might resemble the list in Figure 2-4 below:

Figure 2-4   Preliminary List of Important Facts in Washing Machine Scenario

- Ward bought new washer at Major Appliances, Inc. on 9/30/15.
- Washer came w/1-yr Laundrolux manufacturer's warranty.
- Ward bought additional 2-yr extended warranty from Major Appliances, Inc.
- Washer broke sometime in 7/18.
- Ward mailed claim form on 9/27/18 to Major Appliances, Inc. at address on form; mailed at Ace Hardware P.O. annex; handled by clerk she knew.
- Ward called Major Appliances, Inc. on 10/8/18 b/c had gotten no response.
- Major Appliances, Inc. rep told her Major Appliances, Inc. never received claim & warranty expired on 9/30/18.

Notice that the bulleted list in Figure 2-4 contains some abbreviated phrasing—for example, articles like "a" and "the" are omitted. Most students tend to take notes in shorthand, and this is perfectly acceptable. Just be sure that you can decipher your own notes, because you will need to return to them later.

Looking at the list of facts in Figure 2-4, it is clear that the broad question Ms. Ward's story presents is whether Major Appliances, Inc. is obligated to give Ms. Ward a new washer (or the money to buy one) under the extended warranty.

However, based on your own life experience, and on the fact that your bulleted list includes several specific dates, you should recognize that there is a narrower issue related to the timing of the events. So you might decide that, in addition to your bulleted list of facts, a simple timeline of key dates would be a helpful resource as you move forward with your pre-writing. The timeline for Ms. Ward's situation might look something like the one in Figure 2-5 below:

Figure 2-5	Timeline of Events in Washing Machine Scenario				
9-30-15	9-30-16	July 2018	9-27-18	9-30-18	10-8-18
Purchased machine with 1-year warranty; purchased add'l 2-yr warranty.	1-yr mfg warranty expired.	Machine broke.	Mailed claim form.	Extended warranty expired.	Company denied receiving claim; denied claim b/c warranty had expired.

This timeline does more than just summarize dates; it helps you move toward a narrower issue. As you constructed the timeline, it likely became clear that you need more information about what happened between September 27, when Ms. Ward delivered her form to the postal clerk at Ace, and October 8, when she called Major Appliances, Inc. about the status of her claim. Already, certain questions are likely occurring to you: When was the envelope containing the claim postmarked? What happened to it? Can Major Appliances, Inc. just say, "We didn't get it; end of story"? You intuitively understand that there is more to the story than what you know now, and without knowing "the rest of the story," you are not ready to predict a resolution to your client's problem.◯

Bulleted lists and timelines are common and useful tools for reducing your understanding of the story to a user-friendly format. However, there are other techniques that may work equally well depending on the type of story and your personal preferences. One helpful technique is retelling the story to a fellow student (or even a non-law student). As you retell the story, take written notes about what you include, what you leave out, how you organize the story, what questions the listener asks in response, what new questions occur to you during the retelling, etc.

Putting the facts into narrative form is an especially helpful strategy when your facts don't come to you in a neat package. While the assigning e-mails in this chapter are realistic, they represent only one way your facts might be packaged. Your facts might come to you scattered among several documents; for example, you might receive a file containing a complaint and answer, some depositions, and some affidavits, all of which you must read together to construct the story of the case.◍ Or your facts might come to you in the form of another

◯ Are you writing down these questions as they occur to you? Don't count on yourself to remember them later; they might get away from you before you revisit the problem. If it turns out later that some of the questions you write aren't important to resolving the problem, you can cross them off the list then.

◍ In law school, you're more likely to get a neater package of facts for legal writing assignments, for pedagogical and practical reasons. In practice, you're much more likely to get an assortment of documents from which you will have to extract the story facts. But if you employ the strategies we suggest in this chapter, you should end up with a good written summary of the story, regardless of how the story facts come to you.

attorney's hastily written notes from a meeting with a client. No matter how your facts come to you, developing a narrative of the story in your own words and reducing it to writing will help you (1) remember the salient facts and (2) identify gaps in the story that you'll need to fill as you continue your pre-writing process.

It is extremely important to remember that as you strive to "understand the story," you should not be making final judgments about the significance of the various facts. Don't attempt to categorize facts as "important" or "not important," "helpful" or "not helpful," "relevant" or "irrelevant." It's just too soon. Fact X, which might seem insignificant at this stage, may later turn out to be the crucial fact in resolving the question.

In any scenario, you must avoid the temptation to fill in the blanks in the story on your own by making assumptions about the facts. You should also be cautious about trying to fill in the blanks by simply asking your supervising attorney for more details. While there may be times during your work that it is perfectly appropriate to ask your supervising attorney questions, you don't want to do it too early or too often. Here, it would probably be best to wait to approach Attorney Cox until you have a fuller understanding of the story and a preliminary idea of the narrow issues and the law that governs them.

What is called for here is *patience.*⬤ Rather than trying to fill in the blanks immediately, so that you can hurry to a conclusion, take plenty of time to gather additional facts and to explore the relevant law. As you go through the pre-writing process, you will systematically be moving toward an answer to your question that is based on *solid legal reasoning* rather than on opinion or guesswork.⬤

⬤ Are you in a hurry at this point to resolve the problem? If so, slow down! Patience is a key quality of good lawyers; they understand that ambiguity is preferable to certainty in the early stages of analysis, because it allows for greater exploration of possibilities. You're more likely to arrive at a well-reasoned solution if you keep an open mind, even about the facts, in the early going.

⬤ In previous coursework, you may have been doing just the opposite: beginning with a conclusion and working backwards to "justify it" with your research. Legal analysis simply cannot be done in that order. Legal analysis begins with a question, proceeds through research and analysis, and only then ends with an answer.

Chapter 2 Recap

◯ Every time you undertake a legal analysis, your first product should be this bulleted list. You may be able to do more, but the bulleted list is non-negotiable.

What written product(s) do you now have to assist you as you go forward in your pre-writing process?◯

Segway scenario:
- Bulleted list of aspects of the story that seem important and questions the story raises in your mind.

Washing machine scenario:
- Bulleted list of aspects of the story that seem important and questions the story raises in your mind.
- Timeline of key events.

Where are you in terms of issue formulation?

Segway scenario:
- Broad question: Can the charge against Mr. Byrd stick (did he violate the red-light statute)?
- Preliminary narrow issue: Was the Segway he was riding "a vehicle such as an automobile"?

Washing machine scenario:
- Broad question: Does Major Appliances, Inc. have to honor the extended warranty (give Ms. Ward new washer or $)?
- Preliminary narrow issue: How does the timing of events affect the outcome?

Independent Practice Exercise 2-1

E-MAIL

To:	Junior Associate
From:	Edwin Shore, Senior Partner
Sent:	August 9, 2019
Subject:	Potential Client Rose McMahon
	Enforceability of Covenant Not to Compete

Today I received a phone call from a potential client, Dr. Rose McMahon. Dr. McMahon is an OB/GYN. Dr. McMahon received her medical degree from Wake Forest School of Medicine in 2011. In February 2018, she joined Alleghany Obstetric & Gynecological Associates, P.A. (AOGA), located in Sparta, North Carolina, in Alleghany County. Dr. McMahon grew up in Sparta, and she really wanted to go back home to raise her children and to care for her ailing father. Also, one of her ancestors was a midwife in Sparta many years ago, so Dr. McMahon feels like she really belongs there.

Unfortunately, according to Dr. McMahon, the other three doctors in AOGA, who are all male, treat her unfairly. She claims they generally discriminate against her in various ways. They make her work weekends, and they require her to be on call more often than they are. Initially, she was also paid less than the male doctors, but she is now paid the same. However, she sees more patients, and her billables are higher. She believes the other doctors are jealous of the rapport she has with her patients.

pay discrepancy

Dr. McMahon has repeatedly expressed to her partners her desire to provide free medical care to indigents in the Alleghany County area, but they do not support this desire. So she now wants to start her own practice. Dr. McMahon believes that the market could easily absorb a new OB/GYN practice; aside from AOGA, there is only one other OB/GYN, also a male, who practices alone. He appears to be in his 60s, and Dr. McMahon thinks he may retire before long, though she has nothing specific to back that up. So her separate practice would, initially at least, result in three different OB/GYN practices in the county.

Unfortunately, Dr. McMahon signed a covenant not to compete when she went to work with AOGA. A copy of the covenant is attached. She wants to know if it is enforceable; she feels she could be successful in her own practice because of the good relations she's developed with her patients, but she also doesn't want to lose in court if her colleagues at AOGA try to enforce the covenant.

Main issue

As the copy of the covenant confirms, the other three doctors in the practice never signed it. And Dr. McMahon only printed her name instead of signing it in cursive. She remembers thinking that "the lawyers" were still going to meet with her, but that never happened, for whatever reason. Interestingly, Dr. McMahon also printed her name on the other documents she filled out right before she began her employment: an Employment Agreement, a W-4 (withholding) form, and a form regarding the practice's retirement plan.

Other than Dr. McMahon, the nearest female OB/GYN is at least an hour away from Sparta. Also, Sparta gets snowed in often, sometimes for a day or more at a time, making it hard for pregnant patients to travel. Dr. McMahon has determined that a number of her patients will sign affidavits attesting to their desire to keep seeing Dr. McMahon, but none of the doctors in the county are willing to sign affidavits in her support; they do not want to take sides.

Dr. McMahon heard from a doctor friend in New Bern that covenants not to compete are not valid in North Carolina as to doctors. Although that is a very broad and somewhat inaccurate statement, there are several possible issues regarding the enforceability of this particular covenant, including (1) that Dr. McMahon printed her name; (2) that no one from AOGA signed the covenant; (3) the extent of the time and territory provisions in the covenant; and (4) the public policy ramifications of the covenant.

is the covenant not to compete enforceable?

First determine whether print can legally bind Dr. in this incident

I think our first inquiry should be whether we can establish that the covenant is unenforceable because Dr. McMahon printed her name instead of signing it. If the covenant is void for that reason, we don't need to get into whether the substance of the covenant is valid. Please write a short memo analyzing this issue and e-mail it to me as soon as possible. Dr. McMahon and I have a follow-up phone call on August 15.

* * *

COVENANT AGAINST COMPETITION

Names parties

This Covenant Against Competition ["Covenant"] is entered by and between Alleghany Obstetric and Gynecologic Associates, P.A. ["the Practice"] and Rose McMahon ["Physician"], contemporaneously with the Employment Agreement entered this date by and between the same parties.

determine whether this is enforceable?

In consideration of Physician's employment with the Practice pursuant to the Employment Agreement and the compensation Physician shall receive pursuant to that Employment Agreement, which Physician agrees is sufficient consideration to support the entry of this Covenant, Physician hereby agrees that, if Physician's employment with the Practice is terminated for any reason, Physician will not engage in the practice of medicine in any capacity whatsoever, including without limitation, as a proprietor, partner, investor, shareholder, director, officer, employee, consultant, independent contractor, or otherwise, for a period of two years from the date of such termination, anywhere within the County of Alleghany, North Carolina.

Physician further agrees that any breach of this Covenant shall cause irreparable harm to the Practice that would be difficult to measure monetarily and that the Practice shall therefore be entitled to seek injunctive relief in a North Carolina court to enjoin any such breach.

This 5th day of February 2018.

By:　　Rose McMahon
　　　　Physician
　　　　　　　Rose McMahon
　　　　　　　———————————

By:　　Alleghany Obstetric and
　　　　Gynecologic Associates, P.A.
　　　　———————————

Using the techniques described in this chapter, make (1) a bulleted list of the aspects of Dr. McMahon's story that seem important; (2) additional notes on the story in another format (e.g. a timeline) if you think such notes would be helpful; (3) a statement of the broad question the scenario presents; and (4) the preliminary narrow issue, if you can identify one at this point. You will be revisiting Dr. McMahon's scenario in subsequent exercises throughout the *Handbook*.

Independent Practice Exercise 2-2

Assume you have received the following e-mail from your supervising attorney:

E-MAIL

To: Assistant District Attorney
From: Omari Phillips, District Attorney
Sent: August 9, 2019
Subject: *State v. Clark*
              19-CRS-12289

I need your help with a case we've recently charged. The defendant, Steven Clark, has been charged with first degree burglary. Apparently, Clark broke into a barn that's also used as a game room. He stole some property from Michael Anderson, who owns the barn and the property it's located on. Clark dropped his wallet near the barn and admits to going in there and taking items, so the public defender is going to be pretty limited in what she can argue in Clark's defense.

Attached is a sketch of the layout of the barn, the investigating officer's report, and an affidavit from Clark that the PD sent us. I expect the PD to argue that Clark's actions don't qualify as first degree burglary under North Carolina law. I need you to assess the viability of that argument. I know there are other facts we might need to discover, but for now, you should assume that the facts in the police report and the affidavit are accurate. Please write a memo for the file assessing whether we should proceed with a first-degree burglary prosecution.

Don't worry about preparing a sentencing report yet; we can do that later if we need to.

[Handwritten margin notes: "For Clark"; "Issue — address both"; "will the barn be deemed as a dwelling ho××"; "curtilage?"]

Diagram of Game Room/Barn at 344 Midway Road, Statesville 28677

All open with fencing & gates

Ping Pong Table		Cow Pen	Cow Pen	Chicken Pen
		Hay & Feed Storage		

STATE OF NORTH CAROLINA,
  Prosecution

ARREST REPORT

      v.   File No. 19CRS012289

STEVEN ALEXANDER CLARK,
  Defendant

REPORTING OFFICER:
Francisco Montez

DATE: July 05 2019

On the night of July 04 2019, I responded to a 9-1-1 dispatch call to the residence of Mr. Michael James Anderson, at 344 Midway Road, Statesville, North Carolina, 28677. Upon my arrival at approximately 23:42 (EST), Mr. Anderson told me that he had scared off a burglar. Mr. Anderson said that he was missing two one-thousand-dollar traveler's checks from his personal safe, his personal laptop, his camera, and a rifle he used for hunting.

Personal property / items taken

Mr. Anderson said that he had been sitting on his back porch, enjoying the July 04 fireworks, when he heard a loud ruckus coming from his barn, which is located approximately 40 feet from his home. Mr. Anderson stated that he ran through the backyard, afraid that his cows and chickens were upset from the fireworks. When he entered his barn, he noticed a person wearing a ski mask, a black sweat shirt, black sweat pants, and gray sneakers. This person seemed startled to see Mr. Anderson and ran out through the side door of the barn. Mr. Anderson then noted that the person dropped the bag he/she was carrying as he/she ran from the yard. I asked Mr. Anderson what time he thought the person had entered the barn. He said he did not know. The fireworks began at 22:00 (EST) and ended about forty-five minutes later. Mr. Anderson discovered the intruder upon entering his barn about 5 minutes into the fireworks show.

disguise

I thought

I investigated the bag on the lawn. Inside the canvas bag were a laptop computer, a Nikon camera, and a Garmon G.P.S. I asked Mr. Anderson if these items were his personal property, and he responded yes. Next to the canvas bag, about four feet away, was a wallet. I opened the wallet and discovered a driver's license for a Mr. Steven Alexander Clark, 130 Vine Street, Statesville, NC 28677.

I walked through Mr. Anderson's barn to explore possible modes of entry for the intruder. I noticed that in one portion of the barn, Mr. Anderson had placed a couch, an antique wood stove, a large table with books and papers scattered on it, a ping pong table, and a television. Mr. Anderson stated that his two teenage sons often use this unfinished game room to entertain themselves and their friends. There was one door directly into the game room from the barn and one door that went from the barn to the animal pens. The pens were gated with fencing. None of the doors were damaged. I further discovered that the bolt on one of the animals'

occupancy

gates had been cut, and I surmised the burglar had cut the bolt to gain entry into the barn through the gate. The gate was hanging ajar when I found it. Mr. Anderson stated that the laptop, camera, and G.P.S. had been on the table in the main room of the barn, which is adjacent to the game room. The rifle had been hanging on the wall next to the animal pens.

Mr. Anderson valued the approximate worth of each item as follows:

Apple MacBook Pro laptop computer: $1,500.
Nikon digital SDR camera: $250.
Garmon G.P.S: $300.
Hunting Rifle: $1,500.00.
Currency: $2,000.00 (traveler's checks).

I left Mr. Anderson's residence at approximately 11:55 p.m. (EST) on July 04 2019. The next morning, at approximately 7:00 a.m. (EST) on July 05 2019, I went to the address on the driver's license in the abandoned wallet, 130 Vine Street, Statesville, NC 28677. A man in his late forties answered the door upon my knock. I identified the man as Mr. Steven Alexander Clark by comparing his appearance to the photo on the license. I informed Mr. Clark that I had found his wallet. Mr. Clark did not respond. I asked him if he had lost his wallet. He did not respond. When I asked Mr. Clark why his wallet was at the residence of Mr. Anderson, he again did not respond. I glanced around Mr. Clark's residence through the open door and noticed some traveler's checks on his living room coffee table (approximately ten feet away). At that point, I asked Mr. Clark if I could come in, and he pushed the door aside to allow me to enter. Once inside Mr. Clark's residence, I saw that the traveler's checks bore Mr. Anderson's name and signature and were designated in the amount of one thousand dollars each. At that point, I took Mr. Clark into custody for the burglary of Mr. Anderson's residence.

I certify that the above is true to the best of my knowledge under the penalty of perjury.

F. Montez
Officer Francisco Montez

* * *

STATE OF NORTH CAROLINA,
    Prosecution

ARREST REPORT
File No. 19CRS012289

    v.

STEVEN ALEXANDER CLARK,
    Defendant

STATEMENT OF STEVEN ALEXANDER CLARK
DATE: July 05 2019

I am fifty-six years old and a graduate of Mitchell Community College, where I earned an Associates Degree. I have been working in my auto repair shop for the last 20 years. I can fix about anything that is wrong with a car, truck, motorcycle, or scooter. When I was 18, I married my high school sweetheart, and we now have four children. My youngest child is 10. My wife doesn't work outside of the home because she stayed home to take care of the kids.

We have been making ends meet throughout our marriage, but last month, my oldest child called and needed money to finish her last year in college at Georgia State. We couldn't help her because we've been swamped with medical bills since I don't have very good insurance and I had a heart attack 6 months ago. The hospital said it would negotiate the bill down if I would come up with $3,500. Otherwise, the bill would be over $15,000.

Mr. Anderson had come into the repair shop a week or two ago to have his car serviced. When I checked him out, he paid with a traveler's check. I noticed that in his wallet he had several more checks filled out with the amount of one thousand dollars. I thought if I could go to his house and ask him to borrow some money, he might give me a loan. Mr. Anderson has two sons who are getting ready to go to college, so I thought he might understand my situation.

I went to Mr. Anderson's house on the 4th of July, but just to ask him for a loan. When he didn't answer the front door, I figured he was at the barn with the animals. I drove down the side drive and went down to the barn to see if he was there. The barn door was unlocked, so I went inside, but I didn't see Mr. Anderson anywhere. As I was walking through the game room, I saw a laptop, a camera, two traveler's checks, and a G.P.S. I grabbed a grocery bag and threw all that stuff in it. I don't even know why.

Just as I was about to reconsider taking the property, I saw Mr. Anderson, and I froze. I didn't want the stuff any longer, so I just ran out of the barn and dropped the bag on the lawn. I guess that is when I dropped my wallet. When I got home, I noticed I still had the traveler's checks in my pocket. I had planned to take them back to Mr. Anderson, but then the officer came to my door the next morning.

I have read the above statement and swear, upon penalty of perjury, that the statement is true and accurate.

Signed,

Steven Alexander Clark
Steven Alexander Clark

Using the techniques described in this chapter, make (1) a bulleted list of the aspects of Mr. Clark's story that seem important; (2) additional notes on the story in another format (e.g. a timeline) if you think such notes would be helpful; (3) a statement of the broad question the scenario presents; and (4) the preliminary narrow issue, if you can identify one at this point. You will be revisiting Mr. Clark's scenario in subsequent exercises throughout the *Handbook*.

Independent Practice Exercise 2-3

Assume you have received the following e-mail from your supervising attorney:

E-MAIL

To: Junior Associate
From: Lillian Hale, Senior Attorney
Date: August 9, 2019
Subject: Client Joseph Mordino
File #19-901

Yesterday I had an initial consultation with Mr. Joseph Mordino. He has been sued, along with his employer, The Grand Wailea Hotel (whom we do not represent) in connection with an incident at the Hotel this past August. He was served on July 12, and he just now retained our firm to represent him. I'll get a 30-day extension tomorrow morning when the Clerk's office opens.

Mr. Mordino provided me with a copy of the Complaint filed against him and the Hotel, a copy of which I have attached. I interviewed Mr. Mordino about the facts alleged in the Complaint and, not surprisingly, he disputed many of them. Here's what he told me:

- On June 22, 2019, he was working at the pool known as the "Family Pool" until his shift ended at 8:00 pm.
- At that time, he changed out of his lifeguard uniform and chose to move over to the "Adult Pool" on the Hotel's property to visit with his girlfriend.
- He claims that the plaintiff, Samuel Zelman, did not "strike up a conversation" with several women at the pool, but instead was loudly yelling lewd and disrespectful remarks at the women, including Mr. Mordino's girlfriend.
- He states that when he went over to speak with Mr. Zelman he noticed four empty beer bottles on the side table next to Mr. Zelman, in addition to the one Mr. Zelman was actively drinking.
- He claims that he didn't "loom over" Mr. Zelman but did stand next to the lounge chair in which Mr. Zelman was lying and politely asked him to stop yelling at the women. He states that he said something like, "I think you might have had a little too much to drink, so why don't you go up to your room and sleep it off?"
- He claims that Mr. Zelman declined to leave or stop yelling and told him to "f*** off", asking him, "What are you going to do to stop me?"
- He states that at that point, he placed a hand on Mr. Zelman's shoulder and told him, "I will make you leave if you won't go on your own."

- He claims that Mr. Zelman was clearly intoxicated, could barely stand, and took a swing at him, which is when Mr. Zelman fell to the ground and injured himself.

Please draft a memo analyzing whether Mr. Mordino's employer, the Hotel, is vicariously liable for his conduct if, in fact, it was tortious. Another associate is investigating the assault and battery angle.

I'll need your memo by close of business on Wednesday, September 5. Our 30-day extension will expire on September 10, and I'll need a couple of days to draft a responsive pleading.

Let me know if you have any questions.

* * *

IN THE DISTRICT COURT
OF THE STATE OF HAWAII
MAUI COUNTY
CASE NO. 19-901 SOM/LEK

SAMUEL ZELMAN,
Plaintiff,

v.

JOSEPH MORDINO and GRAND
WAILEA HOTEL, INC.,
Defendants,

COMPLAINT
JURY TRIAL DEMANDED

Plaintiff SAMUEL ZELMAN, through his undersigned attorney, alleges the following:

1. Plaintiff is and was at all relevant times a citizen and resident of the state of Hawaii. Plaintiff resides at 4613 Larwin Avenue, Honolulu, Hawaii.
2. Defendant Joseph Mordino ("Defendant Mordino") is and at all relevant times was a citizen and resident of the state of Hawaii. Defendant resides at 12700 Viking Court, Wailea, Hawaii.
3. Defendant Grand Wailea Hotel, Inc. ("Defendant Hotel") is a corporation organized and existing under the laws of the State of Hawaii with its principal place of business in Wailea, Hawaii.
4. Pursuant to Hawaii Revised Statutes § 634-35, this Court has subject-matter jurisdiction over the claims in this action and personal jurisdiction over Defendants in this action.
5. Defendant Mordino is employed by Defendant Hotel as a lifeguard for the four (4) pools on Defendant Hotel's property. The pools are provided as amenities for use by guests of Defendant Hotel.
6. On June 22, 2019, Plaintiff, then twenty-two (22) years of age, was a guest at Defendant Hotel.

7. After 8:00 pm, there is no lifeguard on duty at the Adult Pool at Defendant Hotel.
8. Plaintiff had been sitting in a lounge chair by the Adult Pool for approximately 90 minutes when Defendant Mordino entered the pool area and sat in a lounge chair beside a female guest who, upon information and belief, was an acquaintance of Defendant Mordino.
9. At approximately 8:30 pm, Plaintiff struck up a conversation with a group of several women at the Adult Pool.
10. Defendant Mordino subsequently walked over to Plaintiff (who was still sitting in his lounge chair), loomed over him, and forcefully asked him to stop talking to the women.
11. Plaintiff declined to stop talking to the women and denied any wrongdoing.
12. Defendant Mordino then put a hand on Plaintiff's shoulder and threatened to make him leave the pool.
13. Plaintiff subsequently stood up to confront Defendant Mordino and tripped over a lounge chair.
14. Plaintiff was treated by Defendant Hotel's medical staff for a dislocated shoulder and a cut on his forehead.
15. Plaintiff complained about Defendant Mordino's conduct to Defendant Hotel, but Defendant Hotel took no action against Defendant Mordino.

COUNT 1
ASSAULT

16. Paragraphs 1-15 are incorporated herein by reference.
17. Defendant Mordino's actions as described herein were carried out with intent to cause Plaintiff to experience a nonconsensual harmful or offensive contact or apprehension thereof.
18. Defendant Mordino's actions as described herein caused Plaintiff to apprehend imminent contact with Defendant Mordino.
19. As a direct and proximate result of Defendant Mordino's conduct, Plaintiff suffered painful and permanent injuries to his person, including, but not limited to, a dislocated shoulder and stiches to his forehead.
20. Plaintiff has incurred and will continue to incur significant medical treatment and expenses resulting from Defendant Mordino's conduct.
21. As a direct and proximate result of Defendant Mordino's conduct, Plaintiff suffered painful and permanent injuries to his person, including, but not limited to, a dislocated shoulder and stitches to his forehead.
22. Plaintiff has incurred and will continue to incur significant medical treatment and expenses resulting from Defendant Mordino's conduct.

COUNT 2
BATTERY

23. Paragraphs 1-22 are incorporated herein by reference.
24. Defendant Mordino's actions as described herein resulted in non-consensual harmful and offensive contact with Plaintiff.

COUNT 3
RESPONDEAT SUPERIOR

25. Paragraphs 1-24 are incorporated herein by reference.
26. Defendant Mordino's actions were conducted within the course and scope of his employment with Defendant Hotel such that Defendant Hotel is liable for the conduct of Defendant Mordino.
27. Defendant Hotel took no action against Defendant Mordino after being informed of his actions against Plaintiff.

WHEREFORE, Plaintiff requests the Court to grant the following relief:

1. Compensatory damages from Defendants, jointly and severally, in an amount in excess of $100,000.
2. Punitive damages from Defendants, jointly and severally, in an amount in excess of $100,000.
3. Attorney's fees and the costs of this action from Defendants, jointly and severally;
4. Such further relief as the Court deems just and proper.

This the 11th day of July, 2019.

_____
Keo Palawuno
Attorney for Plaintiff

* * *

E-MAIL

To: Junior Attorney
From: Lillian Hale, Senior Attorney
Date: August 13, 2019
Subject: Client Joseph Mordino
          File #19-901

I just received a call from the General Counsel of the Grand Wailea Hotel, Mr. Jamie Wingate, and we had an interesting conversation about this case. He received the Complaint this week and wanted to assure us that, as of now, the Hotel has no plans to offer a settlement of any kind. Mr. Wingate also shared some details about Mr. Mordino's employment that I thought might be helpful to know as you begin drafting your memo. Here are those facts:

- There was a sign at the Adult Pool that read "No Lifeguard on Duty after 8pm."

- Part of the job description for a lifeguard at the Hotel includes the handling of unruly guests. The job description permits "the use of the requisite amount of force as befits the situation, within reason."
- Employees of the Hotel are also expected to "behave professionally" at all times.
- There is no written policy about employees using the Hotel facilities after their shifts end, but the Hotel is aware that employees often do so and has done nothing to discourage it.

Remember that there is another associate looking into the assault and battery angle; so keep your focus on whether or not the Hotel would be liable if Mr. Mordino did commit a tort. I hope this new information answers some of your questions. Let me know if you have any additional concerns.

Using the techniques described in this chapter, make (1) a bulleted list of the aspects of Mr. Mordino's story that seem important; (2) additional notes on the story in another format (e.g. a timeline) if you think such notes would be helpful; (3) a statement of the broad question the scenario presents; and (4) the preliminary narrow issue, if you can identify one at this point. You will be revisiting Mr. Mordino's scenario in subsequent exercises throughout the *Handbook*.

Independent Practice Exercise 2-4

Assume you have received the following e-mail from your supervising attorney:

E-MAIL

To: Junior Associate
From: Juan Gutierrez, Senior Associate
Sent: August 15, 2019
Subject: Ally Khan's potential VARA claim

Our potential client, Ally "Alley Cat" Khan, had been out of work, without funds, and couch-surfing through his friends' homes for about six months of the previous year. Recently, as Mr. Khan was walking through the neighborhood where he was staying, he saw a sign outside the Jones-Stewman Museum of Modern Art (J-SMOMA) in Chartwell, Massachusetts, saying that the museum was hiring. He walked inside and found out that all the positions had been filled. Seeing Mr. Khan's disappointment, the museum owner, Leo Upstein, said he would create a job for Mr. Khan and drew up a contract under which Mr. Khan could work as a museum gardener and caretaker.

Even though he had no gardening experience, had never worked in a museum, and wasn't even particularly fond of art, Mr. Khan agreed to the contract. He was not put on the payroll and did not receive any health or other benefits, but he did receive a weekly salary in cash and was told he could take a week or so of unpaid vacation after he had worked for a year. Although it wasn't Mr. Khan's career of choice, the weekly salary sounded good, so Mr. Khan agreed.

J-SMOMA is unique because the entire interior space of the museum is a garden divided into food and flower plantings. As a result, gardeners must landscape both the inside and the outside of the museum.

Mr. Khan's duties as a groundskeeper included cutting the grass, watering the plants, trimming the decorative and functional hedges, and generally being responsible, with the other gardeners, for the health and well-being of the interior and exterior grounds of the museum.

Although he had been asked by Mr. Upstein only to keep the hedges decorative and functional, one day Mr. Khan began trimming one of the hedges and accidentally cut too much off. However, when he looked at the misshapen hedge, he suddenly realized he could make it into an interesting design if he kept trimming, so he did.

The next morning, everyone who came to the museum commented on the interesting new garden "sculpture" Mr. Khan had made. Mr. Upstein heard all the compliments and quickly recognized that the attractive shape could be considered modern art and could bring increased recognition to the museum. As a result, when Mr. Khan came to work that day, Mr. Upstein repeated the compliments to him. Mr. Khan was quite flattered and began thinking of himself as a bit of an artist after receiving such praise.

Mr. Upstein asked Mr. Khan if he would be willing to do a different hedge design every month. He insisted that Mr. Khan could have free rein over what he created and that he had "artistic license" to make his garden sculptures as he liked. Mr. Khan agreed to do so.

After that, attendance at the museum increased dramatically month to month, and a local television station even sent a reporter to J-SMOMA to interview Mr. Khan and Mr. Upstein about the changing hedge designs.

Mr. Upstein was so pleased with the increased attendance and with Mr. Khan's growing fame that he installed engraved plates with the legend "Sculpture by Alley Cat" in front of the areas where Mr. Khan's monthly "shows" were located.

Mr. Upstein did not increase Mr. Khan's pay but told Mr. Khan that, if Mr. Khan would continue producing a new garden sculpture every month, he would be put on the VIP list for museum functions and special events and would receive one free meal a day in the museum's café. Mr. Upstein also provided Mr. Khan with new shears and other garden tools to aid in the creation of his designs.

During this period of time, Mr. Khan became so involved in his new task that he took a few related classes at a local community college, including gardening, sculpture, and a survey class about modern art. In addition, he often worked late into the night after his shift had ended to make the newest sculpture match his "artistic vision." He enjoyed making these sculptures so much that he also began making new garden sculptures more than the once a month Mr. Upstein had originally requested.

After six months of new designs, Mr. Khan created a new sculpture he considered to be his masterpiece. It was multi-dimensional and multi-shaped. He named it "Dia-bollo." Mr. Khan was so taken with his new design that he called his friends and everyone he knew to come see it.

However, for an unknown reason, Mr. Upstein did not care for the new sculpture. After a few days, he directed one of the gardeners to alter it into a simple cube shape, but he did not remove the engraved plate from in front of the altered hedge.

Mr. Khan was devastated about the destruction of his masterpiece and does not want his name associated with the altered sculpture, which he considers to be "ugly and plain." He wants to know if he has any rights under the Visual Artists Rights Act, even though the contours of his employment are rather vague.

Please research and write a memo to the file about Mr. Khan's question and let me know the "short" version of your answer as soon as you can. If Mr. Khan has the right to removal of his name, this should be done ASAP.

Using the techniques you have learned in this chapter, make (1) a bulleted list of the aspects of Mr. Khan's story that seem important; (2) additional notes on the story in another format, e.g., a timeline, if you think such notes would be helpful; (3) a statement of the broad question the scenario presents; and (4) the preliminary narrow issue, if you can identify one at this point. You will be revisiting Mr. Khan's scenario in subsequent exercises throughout the *Handbook*.

Chapter 3

Understanding Your Specific Assignment

As a result of the pre-writing work you've already done, you've begun to "get your bearings" relative to the task before you. You have a fuller understanding of the story that is the basis for your assignment and a preliminary idea of what the narrow issues might be. However, you're not yet ready to dive headfirst into the analysis. There is another key step you must take in order to "get your bearings" relative to the task before you: understanding the parameters of the specific assignment you've been given. In other words, you need to understand exactly what you have been asked to do.

There are several reasons why you should wait until you understand the story before you seek to understand your specific assignment. The first reason is a very practical one: Every legal question comes out of a human story. The story is simply the natural starting point for any legal analysis.

The second reason is more theoretical: Starting with the story encourages you to begin your work by thinking broadly and embracing the possibilities that arise from the facts of the story. If you start with the step of understanding the assignment, you may find yourself focusing more on the restrictions presented by the assignment than on the possible solutions to the legal question. Pre-writing is a *process* that leads to a *product*; so the *process* of understanding the story should precede your examination of the contours of the eventual *product*.

The final reason is pedagogical: You will not learn as much from working on the assignment if your first question is, "What should my finished product look like?" Many law students are expert "teacher-learners." They have found success in the past by simply asking the teacher what he or she expects and then producing exactly that. This approach is unlikely to work well on legal writing assignments. No two legal analyses are alike, and the task of writing a memo or brief involves more than simply "filling in the blanks." While looking at a finished memo may help you understand what your finished product should *look like* at a glance, it will be of no help at all in understanding the *content* — the *analysis* — that your document should communicate.◘

In sum, by focusing first on understanding the story, you emphasize the uniqueness of the question before you; then you can proceed to think about how to express the analysis of that unique question in a form that is predictable and useful to the intended audience.

This brings you to the second step in the pre-writing process: understanding your specific assignment. While the step of understanding the story requires a wide view and consideration of all the possibilities, the step of understanding your specific assignment represents a healthy narrowing of your focus.

Many law students are surprised to realize that the law is often not a set of black-and-white answers that can be determined by a fixed method. More often, it involves applying fluid rules to ambiguous facts. Put another way, legal analysis is more art than science. Thus, as you begin a particular legal writing assignment, you might think of yourself as the "artist of your analysis" and your completed assignment as the "work of art."

For example, if you made your living as a sculptor, you would not think of starting to sculpt (or even buying the materials) without understanding your commission. What specifications are explicitly included in the commission? Does the commission specify a material (bronze, clay, marble, wood)? Does it specify the size? The subject matter? These specifications are the starting point for your work.

As you seek to understand your commission as a legal analyst and writer, there are several questions you should ask. What kind of document, if any, am I being asked to produce? Who is the intended audience for my work? What tone is expected (informal or formal, objective or argumentative, etc.)? Approximately how long should the document be? What is the urgency of the request? Do I drop everything to work on this assignment? Do I have a couple of days? A couple of weeks? By answering these questions early, you can plan and execute your commission more efficiently.

Recall the e-mail you received from Attorney Cox about Mr. Byrd's Segway problem, reprinted below in Figure 3-1:

◘ The sooner you can let go of the notion that there is a "sample memo" out there somewhere that you can "copy," the better. The thought process behind every legal analysis is brand new, and there are no shortcuts to the process. Samples can illustrate helpful structural, stylistic, and formatting guidelines, but you still must decide what content to include within those guidelines.

Figure 3-1   Assigning E-mail from Supervising Attorney in Segway Scenario

---

MEMORANDUM

To: Junior Associate
From: Paula Cox, Senior Partner
Re: Client Arthur Byrd
        Alleged violation of Graburg red-light statute
Date: July 15, 2019

Our client, Arthur Byrd, was ticketed by Officer Jan Sprouse on the public roadway at the intersection of Main Street and Cemetery Road in downtown Salem. Mr. Byrd had just crossed the intersection on a Segway i2 SE. The light in his direction of travel was red. He was using the Segway because he had a sprained ankle and was unable to walk extended distances. He borrowed his neighbor's Segway to run a quick errand to the drugstore.

Mr. Byrd was later charged with violating the State of Graburg's red-light statute. My recollection is that the language of the red-light statute only applies to someone driving "a vehicle such as an automobile." Please write a memo to the file assessing whether this charge can stick. I think the case is calendared for early September, and I need to decide how to advise Mr. Byrd.

Your first step would be to understand the story and make a bulleted list of the key aspects of it, as you learned in Chapter 2 (see Figure 2-2). Then, you need to determine what your commission is in this instance: What is your specific assignment?

Attorney Cox has specified that you are to produce a memo to the file, which typically calls for a somewhat formal tone. Although Attorney Cox has not specified the format or length of the memo, she is likely accustomed to a particular memo format, which you should eventually ascertain and follow,❶ and she needs it to be as long as necessary to thoroughly yet concisely convey your analysis.

The phrase "assessing whether this charge can stick" suggests that your senior partner expects an objective analysis of the legal question followed by a prediction of the likely outcome for Mr. Byrd; you are not being asked to construct an argument for Mr. Byrd.❷

As to urgency, you know that you are approximately six weeks away from Mr. Byrd's court date; so, in order to give Attorney Cox adequate time to decide on a strategy, you should probably get to this assignment as soon as possible.

❶ In law school, your professor will probably be very specific as to format. In practice, you will probably get fewer specifics, and you may have to consult a memo from a different case and use that as a "go-by." In any event, don't get bogged down with formatting details in the early pre-writing stages. What's important now is that you educate yourself about the parameters of your commission so that you are properly focused as you move into the research and analysis of the problem.

❷ Although you might naturally be tempted to take Mr. Byrd's side as you move forward, it would be premature to do so, even though he is your client. As you proceed, remain neutral until you have all of the information you need to be able to predict whether or not the charge will stick.

Just as you did when you were working to understand the story, you should generate a written record of your understanding of the parameters of your specific assignment (your commission). For example, you should note that with a trial date looming in early September, there is some urgency here. You might write down August 1 as a target date for completion; that gives Attorney Cox a month to prepare for trial. In general, you should not be asking, "When is the latest time I can start this assignment?" Instead, you should be asking, "How soon can I get this done, to give maximum flexibility to my very busy senior partner?"

You might create a template for recording the details of your specific assignment; you should develop a template that would work for any kind of assignment. For the office memo requested above, you might construct your template as shown in Figure 3-2 below:

Figure 3-2 Record of Parameters of Specific Assignment

Date of assignment	July 15, 2019
Target completion date	August 1, 2019
Specific document(s) requested	Memo to file
Intended audience of document	Attorney Cox
Tone of document	Objective analysis
Expected length	As short as possible ⓘ
Is there a "go-by" for the specific format?	Yes (consult prior memos to file)

Now, suppose that instead of the e-mail above, you have received this e-mail about Mr. Byrd's situation:

Figure 3-3   E-mail from Supervising Attorney

To: Junior Associate
From: Paula Cox, Senior Partner
Sent: July 15, 2019
Subject: Question re: Graburg red-light statute

A friend of mine was recently ticketed in downtown Salem after he ran a red light at an intersection while he was riding a Segway i2 SE. I looked up the Graburg red-light statute, but all it says is that it applies to someone driving "a vehicle such as an automobile." I'm curious about whether my friend violated the statute. Could you take a look at this and get back to me with your thoughts?

ⓘ In legal writing, the goal is to say what you need to say in as few words as possible. This may be a new habit that you will have to develop. In college, you often had a page requirement, and so your goal was to "fill up" the pages, even if that meant phrasing the same content in different ways to take up space. In legal writing, you may have a court-imposed page limit or word count; and even if you do not, your goal is to convey your analysis fully but concisely. In Mr. Byrd's case, your memo should be as many pages as necessary to convey the analysis, and no more.

The e-mail in Figure 3-3, unlike the e-mail in Figure 3-1, requires only a return e-mail in which you answer the question posed in a correspondingly informal tone. Although the e-mail does not specify the format or length of the expected response, you know that by their nature, e-mails are typically fairly short and direct. The language "I'm curious about whether" suggests that, as with the office memo, you should analyze the issue objectively, not argue for a particular outcome. The e-mail also does not specify the urgency; it does not suggest that you need to drop everything to work on a response, nor does it suggest an open-ended deadline. Don't be afraid to ask for clarification as to the urgency of any particular assignment; here, Attorney Cox likely would not mind you shooting her a quick inquiry as to when she needs a response.

Finally, assume for purposes of this example that you have completed your analysis of Mr. Byrd's situation and have concluded that he did not violate the statute.[1] Assume further that after you submit the memo to the file in Mr. Byrd's case, Attorney Cox follows up with the e-mail in Figure 3-4 below:

Figure 3-4   Follow-Up E-mail from Supervising Attorney

MEMORANDUM

To: Junior Associate
From: Paula Cox, Senior Partner
Sent: August 21, 2019
Re: Client Arthur Byrd
           Alleged violation of red-light statute

Thank you for your excellent memo to the file regarding Mr. Byrd's case. I agree with your conclusion that Mr. Byrd probably did not violate the red-light statute. He has given me the go-ahead to pursue a dismissal of the charge.

Mr. Byrd's case is set for trial on September 4. Accordingly, I need you to draft ⓘ a brief in support of a motion to dismiss the charge. Please have the brief to me at least one week before the trial.

> ⓘ When your senior partner uses the word "draft," she does not mean "rough draft." She expects a product that is as complete, polished, and professional as possible.

---

1. This is purely a hypothetical outcome that we include here for pedagogical purposes. It will take you until the end of Chapter 8 to reach your own answer to Mr. Byrd's question.

In this instance, even though you have already devoted time and effort to understanding the story and analyzing the issue, and you have already produced one document, you still need to determine what your new commission is based on this e-mail. This time, Attorney Cox has specified that you are to produce a trial brief. Your ultimate audience is no longer Attorney Cox (although of course she will be reading it); your ultimate audience is the judge who holds Mr. Byrd's fate in his hands. Thus, your brief must comply with all of the formal requirements for trial briefs in your jurisdiction.

As to format and length, it's very likely that there are specific rules promulgated by the court, and you must follow them. The phrase "draft a brief in support of a motion to dismiss the charge" indicates that Attorney Cox now expects you to craft an argument supporting Mr. Byrd's position that a Segway is not "a vehicle such as an automobile" under the statute. As to urgency, you know that you must have the brief to Attorney Cox by August 28 (one week before the trial), so you have exactly one week to complete the commission.

❶ Note that this is the first time in the life of Mr. Byrd's case that you have been asked to argue his position, and this is only because your careful objective analysis suggested that his argument is valid.

Turning to the washing machine scenario, recall that your firm has been approached by Ms. Ward about Major Appliances, Inc.'s assertion that it did not receive her claim under the extended warranty and therefore does not have to honor the warranty claim. The e-mail you received from Attorney Cox is reproduced below in Figure 3-5.

Figure 3-5   Assigning E-mail from Supervising Attorney

To: Junior Associate
From: Paula Cox, Senior Partner
Sent: October 15, 2018
Subject: Alice Ward's possible breach of warranty claim

This morning I met with a potential client, Ms. Alice Ward. Ms. Ward is a resident of South Carolina who purchased a new Laundrolux washing machine at Major Appliances, Inc. on September 30, 2015. The machine came with a one-year manufacturer's warranty, and Ms. Ward purchased an additional two-year extended warranty on the machine through Major Appliances, Inc. When the machine broke in July 2018, Ms. Ward was too busy to deal with it right away. She finally got around to contacting Laundrolux, who told her to contact Major Appliances, Inc. because the one-year Laundrolux manufacturer's warranty had expired.

On September 27, 2018, Ms. Ward found the extended warranty and the accompanying claim form in her files. She completed the form and put it in an envelope addressed to Major Appliances, Inc. at the address listed on the form. Later that day, she took the envelope to her local Ace Hardware store, which maintains a post office annex. She handed the envelope to the clerk, Maria Jones, who frequently handles Ms. Ward's mail.

Eleven days later, on October 8, 2018, Ms. Ward realized that she had not received a response from Major Appliances, Inc., and she called the local store. When she was finally connected to someone in the warranty department, she was told that Major Appliances, Inc. had never received her claim and that the warranty had expired on September 30, 2018. Ms. Ward cannot afford to buy a new washing machine, and she would like to know whether we can help her enforce the warranty.

I think that this transaction may fall under the common law "mailbox rule." If it does, we may be able to help Ms. Ward. Please look into this matter and draft a letter to Ms. Ward advising her of her options. Ms. Ward has been calling me daily to inquire about the matter, so please get this letter drafted right away.

Mailbox Rule

Client Letter

Your commission here is to write an opinion letter (sometimes called a "client letter") to Ms. Ward. The letter must be appropriately formal, given that Ms. Ward and your firm have a professional relationship. However, because Ms. Ward is not a lawyer, the letter must be written in plain enough language that she can understand its content and meaning. You would probably not reference specific statutes or cases; and if you do, you would probably not cite them in full, as you would if you were writing to another lawyer or to a court.

The basic tone of the opinion letter to Ms. Ward would be objective, in that you are explaining the law and how it applies to the facts of her situation. (If the results of your analysis are unfavorable to Ms. Ward, your tone would still be objective, but you might temper your objectivity with a measure of empathy.) You want to aim for a concise, direct explanation of the results of your analysis, and you want to answer Ms. Ward's question at the outset. As to urgency, this is one instance when you might need to put other tasks on hold and get straight to work; Attorney Cox wants the letter "right away." Once again, your template will enable you to summarize your commission, as shown below in Figure 3-6:

Figure 3-6 Record of Parameters of Specific Assignment

Date of assignment	October 15, 2018
Target completion date	ASAP
Specific document(s) requested	Opinion letter to client
Intended audience of document	Ms. Ward
Tone of document	Objective; accessible to lay audience
Expected length	Short (1-2 pages)
Is there a "go-by" for the specific format?	Yes (ask colleague)

Suppose you determine through research and analysis that Ms. Ward has a viable claim in federal court for breach of warranty against Major Appliances, Inc.,[2] and you e-mail Attorney Cox conveying this result. Suppose further that before you've drafted the opinion letter to Ms. Ward, Attorney Cox calls you,❶ suggesting that in addition to the letter to Ms. Ward, you also draft a demand letter to Major Appliances, Inc. for Ms. Ward's review. Now you have two assignments, each with different parameters.

There will be some similarities between the opinion letter to Ms. Ward and the demand letter to Major Appliances, Inc. Both will be objective in tone, with appropriate formality and professional respect for the recipient; both will convey the same legal analysis. However, the demand letter must do more than convey information clearly and objectively; it must also attempt to persuade Major Appliances, Inc. that its denial of Ms. Ward's claim was erroneous and that Major Appliances, Inc. should therefore act promptly to remedy the error.

This attempt to persuade requires you to be more specific in your description of your analysis, including your citations to the law, especially because the recipient of the letter to Major Appliances, Inc. is likely a fellow lawyer. In fact, it might benefit you to tackle the letter to Major Appliances, Inc. first; after writing the more specific version of the analysis, you will have a clearer understanding of Ms. Ward's legal position, which will likely make it easier to draft the opinion letter to her. Your template can be easily modified to include both assignments, since they are related.

❶ While your law school assignments usually come to you in written form, understand that in practice, that is not always the case. Sometimes assignments will be conveyed in a phone call, in an encounter in the hallway, or even in a text. Regardless of how the assignment is conveyed to you, your approach to getting your bearings should be the same: understand the story, and then understand your commission.

---

2. Again, you won't know the answer to Ms. Ward's question until Chapter 8. Here, we are presupposing an answer for pedagogical purposes.

In any scenario, the primary purpose of this step in the pre-writing process is to reduce to writing the concrete requirements of your commission. However, a secondary purpose should always be to determine whether the assignment itself contains any information that limits the scope of the questions you will need to analyze.

For example, going back to the Segway scenario, suppose that in addition to being criminally charged under the Graburg red-light statute, Mr. Byrd has also been sued for civil damages by a pedestrian he hit in the crosswalk. Ideally, Attorney Cox would include in her memo to you a limiting instruction such as: "By the way, Jane Morgan is already looking into the civil matter, so you should focus only on the criminal charges." If she does not include such an instruction, and you know that Mr. Byrd hit a pedestrian in the intersection, you would be wise to seek clarification of the scope of your commission.

When your commission has such limitations, make sure you include that information on your template, as shown in Figure 3-7 below:

Figure 3-7   Record of Parameters of Specific Assignment

Date of assignment	July 15, 2019
Target completion date	August 1, 2019
Specific document(s) requested	Memo to file
Intended audience of document	Attorney Cox
Tone of document	Objective analysis
Expected length	No limit
Is there a "go-by" for the specific format?	Yes (consult prior memos to file)
Limitations on scope of analysis	Do not address civil liability to injured pedestrian

Other possible limitations may arise where there are multiple parties on the same side of the case (should your analysis focus on just one of the parties, or on all of them?) or where there is more than one discrete legal question (a products liability claim and a statute of limitations question under the same set of facts—should you analyze both, or has your supervising attorney limited the assignment to one question only?). Maintain flexibility in using your template, so that you clearly capture any limitations.

○ You MUST AVOID the temptation to "improvise" or modify the facts to create questions that aren't there. Law students are particularly susceptible to this temptation; it is often a fun intellectual exercise to hypothesize about how a case would come out under different facts. In fact, your law school professors will often ask you to do exactly that as a means of exploring the limits of a legal principle. However, when you are tackling a specific legal writing assignment, this kind of hypothesizing can complicate the process and, even worse, can obscure the proper focus of your commission.

○ Be encouraged that with practice, you will get better at these steps, and they generally won't take as much time as they do now. Take a moment to reflect on the progress you have already made, even at this early stage in your pre-writing!

Many assignments will not involve such limitations; but if an assignment does, you certainly want to know that before you begin your research and analysis. Even where your assignment does not include explicit limitations, you want to take care not to make extra work for yourself by creating questions that are not raised by the story.○ For example, if your client was involved in a slip-and-fall while shopping in a store, you need only analyze the store's potential liability toward its customers; there is no need to consider what the store's potential liability would be *if* your client had been a trespasser.

It is important for you to recognize that the steps involved in "getting your bearings"—understanding the story and understanding your specific assignment—simply pave the way for your eventual legal analysis. You may be tempted to leap ahead toward making a conclusion about the outcome of your situation; do not give in to temptation! While these early pre-writing steps may seem to make for slow going,○ they are essential in helping you be sure that you are very clear about what you should be focusing on as you proceed to the next stage in the pre-writing process: locating and reading the relevant authorities.

Chapter 3 Recap

What written product(s) do you now have to assist you as you go forward in your pre-writing process?

Segway scenario:
- Bulleted list of aspects of the story that seem important and the questions the story raises in your mind.
- *Completed template summarizing parameters of specific assignment(s).*

Washing machine scenario:
- Bulleted list of aspects of the story that seem important and the questions the story raises in your mind.
- Timeline of key events.
- *Completed template summarizing parameters of specific assignment(s).*

Where are you in terms of issue formulation?

Segway scenario:
- Broad question: Can the charge against Mr. Byrd stick (did he violate the red-light statute)?
- Preliminary narrow issue: Was the Segway he was riding "a vehicle such as an automobile"? ◐

Washing machine scenario:
- Broad question: Does Major Appliances, Inc. have to honor the extended warranty (give Ms. Ward new washer or $)?
- Preliminary narrow issue: How does the timing of events affect the outcome? ◐

> ◐ Note that in both of these scenarios, understanding the parameters of your specific assignment does not enable you to refine your issues any further than you did in Chapter 2. But stay tuned!

Independent Practice Exercise 3-1

Return to the e-mail and accompanying documents you received from your supervising attorney regarding Dr. McMahon's scenario, found on pages 16–19. <u>What are the parameters of your specific assignment?</u> Using the template suggested in this chapter (or your own template), record your understanding of your commission. Your recorded notes about your commission should be separate from your bulleted list of the important aspects of Dr. McMahon's story. You will return to both sets of notes as you complete Independent Practice Exercise 4-1 at the end of Chapter 4.

[handwritten note: Use records of parameter of special assign]

Independent Practice Exercise 3-2

Return to the e-mail and accompanying documents you received from the District Attorney regarding Mr. Clark's scenario, found on pages 19–22. What are the parameters of your specific assignment?

Using the template suggested in this chapter (or your own template), record your understanding of your commission. Your recorded notes about your commission should be separate from your bulleted list of the important aspects of Mr. Clark's story. You will return to both sets of notes as you complete Independent Practice Exercise 4-2 at the end of Chapter 4.

Independent Practice Exercise 3-3

Return to the e-mail you received from your supervising attorney regarding Mr. Mordino's scenario, found on pages 23–27. What are the parameters of your specific assignment? Using the template suggested in this chapter (or your own template), record your understanding of your commission. Your recorded notes about your commission should be separate from your bulleted list of the important aspects of Mr. Mordino's story. You will return to both sets of notes as you complete Independent Practice Exercise 4-3 at the end of Chapter 4.

Independent Practice Exercise 3-4

Return to the e-mail you received from your supervising attorney regarding Mr. Khan's scenario, found on pages 27–29. What are the parameters of your specific assignment? Using the template suggested in this chapter (or your own template), record your understanding of your commission. Your recorded notes about your commission should be separate from your bulleted list of the important aspects of Mr. Khan's story. You will return to both sets of notes as you complete Independent Practice Exercise 4-4 at the end of Chapter 4.

Chapter 4

Formulating a Research Plan

As you move into the next stage of your pre-writing process—locating and reading the relevant authorities—you may notice that your approach to this stage has some important parallels to your work in the "getting your bearings" stage. As in that stage, you should begin here by taking a wide view of the possibilities as you formulate a research plan.○ Then, as your plan develops, you can narrow your view again to help you focus your research to match your specific commission.

○ Avoid at all costs the temptation to dive into your research without a plan! The plan may be simple or more complex depending on your commission, but without it, you won't be able to work at maximum efficiency.

Beginning with the broad view, your first step in formulating a research plan is to brainstorm about what you hope to learn from your research. A good place to start your brainstorming is to review the notes on the story that you took at the beginning of your pre-writing process. Recall that those notes gave rise to some key questions to explore as you research.

Returning to the Segway scenario, recall the bulleted list of notes you compiled as you were seeking to understand the story, reprinted below in Figure 4-1:

Figure 4-1   Preliminary List of Important Facts in Segway Scenario

- Mr. Byrd was riding a borrowed Segway.
- He was on a specific errand (not recreational riding).
- He was riding the Segway because he had a sprained ankle.
- He was riding directly on the street (not on sidewalk, driveway, inside, etc.).
- He was downtown (greater likelihood of vehicle/pedestrian traffic).

- He went through a red light.
- He's been charged with violating Graburg red-light statute, which applies to "a vehicle such as an automobile."
- Find out more about the Segway i2 SE.

A quick look through the items on your list should help you generate a number of key research questions, which you should write down. Your list might look like the one in Figure 4-2 below:

Figure 4-2   List of Research Questions for Segway Scenario

- What is the full text of the Graburg red-light statute?
- Are there any cases that clarify why the Graburg legislature made the automobile the basis for comparison?
- Are there any cases discussing the characteristics of an automobile that were important to the legislature when it crafted the statute?
- Are there any cases that discuss whether a Segway is "a vehicle such as an automobile" under the statute and why or why not?
- Do any cases discuss the application of the red-light statute to other modes of transportation? (Here you might actually jot down some other modes of transportation — mopeds, bicycles, baby strollers, skateboards, etc.)

This last question — whether there are cases about other modes of transportation — is especially important. It is possible that you won't find any Graburg cases at all discussing a Segway; if you don't, the only way you can answer your question is to study the characteristics of other vehicles that caused the court to decide they were like or unlike an automobile and then analogize those vehicles to a Segway.[1] Even if you do find one or more Segway cases from other jurisdictions, it would still be helpful to understand how Graburg courts have applied the Graburg red-light statute to other modes of transportation.

You might need to add one further question to your list:

- What are the characteristics of a Segway i2 SE?

This question should be on your list simply because you most likely don't have the specific knowledge about the Segway i2 SE that would permit you to make a helpful comparison between the Segway and an automobile. You may have seen a commercial about the Segway, or you may have even ridden one at some point. But your eventual

---

1. This is called analogical reasoning, which is discussed in Chapters 7 and 8 of the *Handbook*.

analysis cannot be based only on your own personal experience with the Segway, whatever it might be. Your analysis must be based on actual verified facts about the characteristics of the particular Segway model in question—the Segway i2 SE. So your research plan should include a visit to the official Segway internet site or some other reliable source of information.

Another brainstorming technique might be to read some secondary authority that discusses the broad topic(s) of your particular scenario. For example, as you develop your research plan for the Segway question, you might consult one or more treatises covering transportation law, motor vehicle law, and traffic regulation. If the treatise states, "Almost all fifty states have a statute regulating the progress of motor vehicle traffic through intersections with traffic lights," this is a clue that there is likely to be case law from many jurisdictions that could be helpful. If the treatise places heavy emphasis on the policies behind traffic regulations, you can infer that your research and analysis should include policy considerations such as safety, and you might work the term "safety" into a research query somewhere along the way.

While brainstorming can take any number of forms, it is essential that you resist the temptation to "censor" or "filter" your thinking. True brainstorming proceeds from the assumption that all ideas start out equal. Often, our natural tendency is to start criticizing certain ideas before they've had a chance to fully form. A good way to avoid this un-helpful and perhaps dangerous censoring, whether you are brainstorming alone or in a group, is to write down every single idea that emerges before any of them are discussed, criticized, or rejected.

For example, suppose that as you are brainstorming about different kinds of vehicles to research, you think about an airplane. Your first thought is likely to be a censoring thought: "No, an airplane would never be going through a red light at a street intersection, so forget that." However, if you write it down anyway and allow yourself time to examine the idea uncritically, you might realize that there could be some value in briefly exploring airplane cases; perhaps you would come across a case that discusses the differences between airplanes and gliders, and this discussion might somehow inform your Segway analysis. The point is that at this stage, you want to remain as open-minded as possible. Don't "shoot down" your own or someone else's ideas without letting them fully develop.

Once your brainstorming has resulted in a written list of possible questions for exploration, it is time to narrow your focus before finalizing your research plan. As in the "getting your bearings" stage, there may be certain aspects of your specific assignment that will help you refine your research plan. You should consider, for example:

- whether your assignment involves the interpretation of a statute, in which case the statute should be among the very first authorities you consult, if not the first;

- whether your issue is governed by federal law or state law (or both);

- what jurisdiction's law is mandatory as to your issue;

- whether the assignment itself refers to particular legal authorities (if so, they should be among the first authorities you examine); and

- whether there is already authority from your jurisdiction that directly answers your question. (This is rarely the case with a legal writing assignment, but it is certainly possible in practice.)

In the Segway scenario, you know that your question is a matter of Graburg state law,[2] that it involves a Graburg statute, and that cases from Graburg appellate courts would be mandatory authority. Now you are ready to craft a tentative research plan, which you should write down. Your research plan for the Segway scenario might look something like the one in Figure 4-3 below:

Figure 4-3   Research Plan for Segway Scenario

1. Look up Graburg red-light statute; does it define "vehicle such as auto" and does definition help me?
2. Does the statute have annotations that contain research leads?
3. Look for Graburg cases that discuss whether Segway is vehicle such as auto under red-light statute. (If yes, then probably no need for further research.)
4. If no, go to secondary sources to look for persuasive authority directly on point (from other states or fed courts).
5. Look for Graburg cases about other vehicles discussed in connection w/red-light statute. Possible vehicles to look for: moped, motorcycle, airplane, skateboard, bicycle.○
6. Look for Segway cases from other jurisdictions.
7. Look for cases in other jurisdictions about other vehicles (see above list).

○ Never assume that your list is exhaustive; in your research, you may well find helpful cases involving vehicles you hadn't even thought of.

As you move into the next stage of your pre-writing, keep your research plan handy, so that you can adjust it as you find new leads.

This same strategy for formulating a research plan should serve your purposes regardless of the nature or complexity of your assignment. If you were formulating a research plan for the washing

---

2. Obviously, Graburg is not a real jurisdiction, so the entire research plan set forth here is contrived.

machine scenario, for example, you would still begin by taking a broad view of the situation and brainstorming about what you hope to learn from your research. Recall that when you first looked into this story, you created a bulleted list of seemingly important facts, reprinted in Figure 4-4 below:

Figure 4-4   Preliminary List of Important Facts in Washing Machine Scenario

- Ward bought new washer at Major Appliances, Inc. on 9/30/15.
- Washer came w/1-yr Laundrolux manufacturer's warranty.
- Ward bought additional 2-yr extended warranty from Major Appliances, Inc.
- Washer broke sometime in 7/18.
- Ward mailed claim form on 9/27/18 to Major Appliances, Inc. at address on form; mailed at Ace Hardware P.O. annex; handled by clerk she knew.
- Ward called Major Appliances, Inc. on 10/8/18 b/c had gotten no response.
- Major Appliances, Inc. rep told her Major Appliances, Inc. never received claim & warranty expired on 9/30/18.

You then created a timeline capturing the key dates from the scenario, reprinted below in Figure 4-5:

Figure 4-5   Timeline of Events in Washing Machine Scenario

9-30-15	9-30-16	July 2018	9-27-18	9-30-18	10-8-18
Purchased machine with 1-year warranty; purchased add'l 2-yr warranty.	1-yr mfg warranty expired.	Machine broke.	Mailed claim form.	Extended warranty expired.	Company denied receiving claim; denied claim b/c warranty had expired.

After reviewing your bulleted list and your timeline, your brainstorming about the washing machine scenario might result in a list of questions to explore as you research, similar to the one below in Figure 4-6:

Figure 4-6   List of Research Questions for Washing Machine Scenario

- Assuming Major Appliances, Inc. is telling the truth (that it didn't receive Ms. Ward's claim), is Ms. Ward out of luck on her claim?
- If Ms. Ward can prove that the claim was mailed on September 27, does that help her?
- Are there statutes that govern warranty claims?
- Are there cases that address similar situations?

Remember to consult secondary sources to help you understand the "lay of the land" regarding the law about enforcing warranties. This step would be especially important here, because the chances are good that you will not have studied enough contract law yet to know whether this scenario is governed by common law, by statutory law, or by some combination.

Also remember that you should not be "filtering" or "censoring" your thinking at this point. Go ahead and write down all of the questions that occur to you; you can edit your list of questions later if you decide some of them are not important.

At this point, before you finalize your research plan, you should narrow your focus by asking the same kinds of questions listed above for the Segway scenario:

- Where (in what jurisdiction) will my case be heard? Where will I find mandatory authority?
- Does my assignment reference any specific legal authorities, such as statutes or cases? (If so, I need to look at those first.)

In the washing machine scenario, the only helpful information you have right now in this regard is that Ms. Ward resides in South Carolina and that her dispute is with a nationwide company, Major Appliances, Inc. Attorney Cox did not reference any specific authorities in her memo to you, but she did allude to the "common-law mailbox rule." With so little information, you will have to begin by searching broadly for authority that relates to the enforcement of warranties. Your plan should probably begin with some steps designed to help you figure out what jurisdiction's law is mandatory, so that you can tailor your search appropriately.

Now you're finally ready to write down a tentative research plan, which might look like the one in Figure 4-7:

Figure 4-7   Research Plan for Washing Machine Scenario

1. Consult secondary sources (treatises, etc.) to learn more about the enforcement of warranty claims generally. See what research leads this generates.
2. What is the "common law mailbox rule" that my senior partner referred to in the assignment?
3. Look for potentially controlling statutes (federal and state) on enforcement of warranty and timing of notice of warranty claim.
4. Look for cases (federal and state)[3] on enforcement of warranty that focus on timing of notice of warranty claim.
5. Skim cases that seem important to see if they provide further research leads (e.g. references to Supreme Court cases, references to cases from other circuits, etc.).

You may sometimes feel that you are not really accomplishing anything significant by taking the time to formulate a research plan; you may feel that it would be more efficient to just begin the research and see where it takes you. You may be accustomed to beginning your research in a particular area by simply jumping on the internet and seeing what you find, and this strategy may have served your purposes fairly well. However, in spite of the easy access to Lexis, Westlaw, Bloomberg, and other law databases that you now have, the "Google approach" to legal research does not usually produce accurate or thorough results and is not usually efficient in terms of time. By taking the time to work through the *process* of formulating a research plan, you will sharpen your focus in a way that will lead you more directly (and more quickly) to the most relevant authorities.

---

3. If federal law governs, Fourth Circuit cases are mandatory authority, because South Carolina is one of the states included within that circuit. If you had not yet learned this in your legal research class, your first step would be to determine which circuit's opinions are mandatory for federal claims arising in South Carolina.

Chapter 4 Recap

What written product(s) do you now have to assist you as you go forward in your pre-writing process?

Segway scenario:
- Bulleted list of aspects of the story that seem important and the questions the story raises in your mind.
- Completed template summarizing parameters of specific assignment(s).
- *Tentative research plan.*

Washing machine scenario:
- Bulleted list of aspects of the story that seem important and the questions the story raises in your mind.
- Timeline of key events.
- Completed template summarizing parameters of specific assignment(s).
- *Tentative research plan.*

Where are you in terms of issue formulation?

Segway scenario:
- Broad question: Can the charge against Mr. Byrd stick (did he violate the red-light statute)?
- Preliminary narrow issue: Was the Segway he was riding "a vehicle such as an automobile"?❶

Washing machine scenario:
- Broad question: Does Major Appliances, Inc. have to honor the extended warranty (give Ms. Byrd new washer or $)?
- Preliminary narrow issue: How does the timing of events affect the outcome?❶

❶ Note that in both of these scenarios, developing a research plan does not enable you to refine your issues any further than you did in Chapter 2. However, your work at this step is bringing you ever closer to further refinement of the issues.

Independent Practice Exercise 4-1

Return to your notes about Dr. McMahon's story and the commission you were given in connection with it. Brainstorm about the potential research you will need to do to complete your commission. Generate a broad list of key questions the story and the commission raise in your mind. If you think it would be helpful, read some secondary authority. What are the broad contours of the law that you already think you might need to learn about? Finally, generate a narrower list of questions and finalize your research plan. Put that research plan in written form and set it aside to return to at the end of Chapter 5.

Independent Practice Exercise 4-2

Return to your notes about Mr. Clark's story and the commission you were given in connection with it. Brainstorm about the potential research you will need to do to complete your commission. Generate a broad list of key questions the story and the commission raise in your mind. If you think it would be helpful, read some secondary authority. What are the broad contours of the law that you already think you might need to learn about? Finally, generate a narrower list of questions and finalize your research plan. Put that research plan in written form and set it aside to return to at the end of Chapter 5.

Independent Practice Exercise 4-3

Return to your notes about Mr. Mordino's story and the commission you were given in connection with it. Brainstorm about the potential research you will need to do to complete your commission. Generate a broad list of key questions the story and the commission raise in your mind. If you think it would be helpful, read some secondary authority. What are the broad contours of the law that you already think you might need to learn about? Finally, generate a narrower list of questions and finalize your research plan. Put that research plan in written form and set it aside to return to at the end of Chapter 5.

Independent Practice Exercise 4-4

Return to your notes about Mr. Khan's story and the commission you were given in connection with it. Brainstorm about the potential research you will need to do to complete your commission. Generate a broad list of key questions the story and commission raise in your mind. If you think it would be helpful, read some secondary authority. What are the broad contours of the law that you already think you might need to learn about? Finally, generate a narrower list of questions and finalize your research plan. Put that research plan in written form, and set it aside to return to at the end of Chapter 5.

Chapter 5

Incorporating Research into Your Pre-Writing Process

In Chapter 4, you learned about the importance of formulating a research plan as part of your pre-writing process.❶ Once that research plan is in place, you can begin your research. In this chapter, we do not attempt to offer detailed instructions on how to conduct legal research; there are many excellent legal research texts that go step-by-step through the process of legal research, and you most likely are receiving direct instruction in legal research methods. Here we intend only to suggest strategies for effectively incorporating legal research into your pre-writing process.

As an initial matter, you should not begin your research without having a carefully constructed method for keeping track of your work. Your method may be very formal, or you may prefer a more informal method. At this stage of your legal education, when legal research is still a new skill, the better approach might be to use a more detailed and formal method of recording your research path.❶

For example, you could develop your own template for recording your research and use it each time you embark on research for a particular assignment. A sample template follows:

❶ Remember that the plan should be treated as a flexible tool to guide you through your research process and may need adjusting as you progress.

❶ In this step of your pre-writing process, you will start with a written form and fill it in; this differs from previous steps in the pre-writing process, where the written notes come *after* you have thought about the ideas that come to your mind during that stage.

Figure 5-1 Template for Recording Research Results for a Single Issue[1]

Authority (case, statute, secondary, etc.)	Mandatory? (yes or no) If not, why not?	How was authority located (search term, query, references in other source, etc.)?	Helpful? (yes or no)	If helpful, why? If not helpful, why not?	Notes for follow-up

Other widely-used methods of recording research include (1) keeping a formal research log and (2) using a cover sheet to notate each source that you decide to print. You might experiment with several different methods to determine what works best for you. If you find yourself continually asking, "Have I checked this source out already?" you may need to beef up your note-taking so that you can continue to move forward with your plan instead of going around in circles.

In the same vein, it is important that your notes include authorities that you initially deem not helpful. Later, as you move from recording your research path to carefully reading what you've found, you can briefly skim these "not helpful" authorities to confirm that they are "not helpful." At that point, you can confidently continue your work without

---

1. Generally, it is best to use a separate template for each issue you are researching. Trying to record your research results for multiple issues on a single template will likely be frustrating, and it will result in a disorganized and unhelpful set of notes. It will also make it more difficult for you to find specific information when you need it later.

returning to those authorities; in fact, to make sure you don't waste any more time on the "not helpful" authorities, you might want to revise your research notes, so that they only include the helpful authorities.

Using the suggested template for recording your work as you go, your recorded research notes for the Segway scenario might look like the notes in Figure 5-2 below:

Figure 5-2   Sample Record of Segway Research Results[2]

Authority (case, statute, secondary, etc.)	Mandatory? (yes or no) If not, why not?	How was authority located (search term, query, references in other source, etc.)?	Helpful? (yes or no)	If helpful, why? If not helpful, why not?	Notes for follow-up
16 Graburg Gen. Stat. § 2345 (2016).	Yes.	Referenced in e-mail from Attorney Cox.	Yes, very.	It is the governing statute for Mr. Byrd's issue (he was charged w/violating it).	
Shipley v. State of Graburg, 872 S.E.2d 278 (Gra. Ct. App. 2017).	Yes.	Found in annotations to Graburg red-light statute.	Yes.	Addresses how statute applies to toy scooter. One of only two cases interpreting statute.	
Monroe v. State of Graburg, 872 S.E.2d 425 (Gra. Ct. App. 2017).	Yes.	Found in annotations to Graburg red-light statute.	Yes.	Addresses how statute applies to moped. One of only two cases interpreting statute.	

Similarly, your recorded research notes for the washing machine scenario might eventually look like the notes in Figure 5-3 below:

---

2. The Segway scenario involves a set of fictional authorities that are included in full in Chapter 6. For pedagogical reasons, some first-year legal writing assignments are closed-research assignments — that is, the authorities you can use are limited and are specified for you in the assignment. Because the authorities in the Segway scenario are fictional, there is not actually an annotated Graburg statute. We include this only to illustrate that looking at an annotated statute is frequently a good way to find relevant case law interpreting any statute.

Figure 5-3   Sample Record of Washing Machine Research Results[3]

Authority (case, statute, secondary, etc.)	Mandatory? (yes or no)[4] If not, why not?	How was authority located (search term, query, references in other source, etc.)?	Helpful? (yes or no)	If helpful, why? If not helpful, why not?	Notes for follow-up
89 A.L.R. 5th 319	No; secondary source.	A.L.R. database; natural language query: "timing of buyer's notice of breach of warranty."	Yes.	Background; identification of relevant statute.	
U.C.C. § 2-607(3)(a)	No?	Referenced in A.L.R.	Not really?	Seems to refer only to buyer vs. original seller. Does Major Appliances, Inc. still "own" warranty?	Check to see if S.C. has adopted.
Rosenthal v. Walker, 111 U.S. 185, 193 (1884)	Yes.	T & C query: "mailbox" and "mailbox rule."	Yes. Supreme Court.	Contains rule about mailing vs. receipt.	Old case; check for newer case.
S.C. Code Ann. § 36-1-202	Yes.	Natural language search in SC database "receiving notice in commercial transaction."	Yes. South Carolina U.C.C.	Includes definitions of how notice is given and received in commercial transactions.	
White v. Holiday Kamper & Boats, 2008 WL 4155663	No. Unpublished; trial court decision.[5]	T & C query: "breach of warranty" w/100 "S.C. UCC."	Yes, very.	Directly on-point, though at another stage of transaction (revoking sale vs. end of warranty). Does this matter?	

 Recall that Attorney Cox used this term in her initial e-mail to you. That fact alone tells you that the act of mailing the form is probably significant. When you are generating search terms, use every available source of help.

3. Some of the terms in this example (A.L.R., T & C query, etc.) may be unfamiliar to you, given that you are just beginning to learn the specifics of legal research. Our goal here is simply to illustrate what kinds of things you might record and what form the recording might take.

4. Whether a particular authority is mandatory depends on a number of factors, and a detailed explanation of these factors is beyond the scope of the *Handbook*. The washing machine scenario involves a federal court's interpretation of a state law statute; your professor will likely explain to you why this is so and how it affects the weight of the various authorities.

5. As you will learn in your legal research instruction, some opinions are not officially reported, i.e. "unpublished." This may affect their precedential value; many jurisdictions allow them to be cited as authority in limited circumstances. It's worth a quick check of your jurisdiction's rules to find out its policy on citing unpublished opinions; you would not want to base your entire analysis on an un-

One temptation to which many beginning (and some veteran) legal researchers succumb is losing themselves in "database heaven." In other words, they cannot resist the urge to veer off of the main path to explore every side path they come across. For example, while looking for cases related to the Segway scenario, you might see a news story about the inventor of the Segway and his plans for a new invention: a mini-rocket. "That's cool," you think to yourself. "I wonder whether a mini-rocket like that would be commercially available." And before you know it, you've lost your focus on whether a Segway is a vehicle such as an automobile. You're way off the main path; while the possibility of mini-rocket travel is fascinating, it is highly unlikely that a mini-rocket driver will ever be ticketed for running a red light in Graburg. The note-taking process is a disciplinary tool to help you rein in your impulses to veer off the main path.

Another temptation common to beginning legal researchers is to continue to gather sources without periodically pausing to skim the sources. There are several reasons that periodic skimming is valuable. First, it keeps you on your path by allowing you to weed out irrelevant material on a continuing basis. Second, it allows you to find additional research leads within the relevant material. Third, it helps you begin to see the connections between the authorities you are finding.❶ And finally, on a more practical note, it allows you to save trees by helping you make good decisions as to which sources you need to print.

❶ For example, if you took the time to skim the authorities listed in Figure 5-3 during your research process, you would likely notice that the answers to the questions posed by the washing machine scenario require consideration of both the common law of contracts and the applicable sections of the South Carolina version of the Uniform Commercial Code (U.C.C.).

As you move through your research, and your list of relevant authorities grows, you can increase the efficiency of your pre-writing process by preliminarily organizing the authorities according to a number of considerations: Which authorities are mandatory in your jurisdiction? Which authorities are directly on point? How recent are the authorities? Do the authorities address the same issues or different issues? This might be a mental exercise at this point; or, if you have printed out (or kept an electronic file of) a number of authorities, you might consider physically arranging them into categories that will help you read them more efficiently later.

This preliminary organization has the added benefit of helping you recognize gaps in your research. Suppose you pause as you are researching to assess and preliminarily organize the relevant authorities you've found, and you discover that you have found nothing that fits in the "mandatory authority" category. This could mean either that there is no mandatory authority relevant to your question, or that you have not been thorough in your research and have missed

---

published opinion without confirming that your court will accept that opinion as authority. In the federal court system, trial court decisions are not binding on other trial courts.

important mandatory authority. Or suppose you are researching whether the three elements of a statute have been met, and your preliminary organization reveals that you have found relevant authority on only two of the elements. In this situation you know that your research is incomplete.

Not every gap can be identified at this stage of the pre-writing process; in fact, some gaps do not show up until the writing process is underway. But pausing now to identify obvious gaps is worthwhile, because it gets you further down the path toward finding your answer. And, if you do discover any gaps, you need to stop and fill them before you continue your pre-writing process. Your goal is to be able to move through your reading of the authorities without having to interrupt your thinking to go back to the library or database to conduct more research.

If, after careful consideration, you determine that there are no obvious gaps in your research and that the sources you've skimmed are likely to lead to the answer to your question, you are ready to conclude the research phase of your pre-writing process. One of the most difficult decisions a beginning researcher faces is the decision to stop researching and begin reading and analyzing. There are several reasons why.

First, most law students (and lawyers) enjoy researching; it can be fun to get lost in "database heaven." Second, many students are fearful that they have missed "The Case" — the one source that provides the absolute answer to the question. As you will learn quickly, in most scenarios "The Case" doesn't exist! And third, it's easier to keep "finding" authorities than it is to begin the hard work of reading and assessing them.

However, if you have (1) followed a good research plan, (2) used the strategies your legal research professor has taught you, (3) kept a good record of your work, (4) preliminarily organized your work and assured yourself that there are no obvious gaps in your research, and (5) determined that you have indeed found authorities that will lead to an answer to your question, you can — and should — confidently move forward to the next step in your pre-writing process: reading and assessing the relevant authorities.

Chapter 5 Recap

What written product(s) do you now have to assist you as you go forward in your pre-writing process?

Segway scenario:
- Bulleted list of aspects of the story that seem important and the questions the story raises in your mind.
- Completed template summarizing parameters of specific assignment(s).
- Tentative research plan.
- *Record of research results.*

Washing machine scenario:
- Bulleted list of aspects of the story that seem important and the questions the story raises in your mind.
- Timeline of key events.
- Completed template summarizing parameters of specific assignment(s).
- Tentative research plan.
- *Record of research results.*

Where are you in terms of issue formulation?

Segway scenario:
- Broad question: Can the charge against Mr. Byrd stick (did he violate the red-light statute)?
- Preliminary narrow issue: Was the Segway he was riding "a vehicle such as an automobile"?
- *Note: I didn't find any Segway cases; the cases address two other "vehicles" (toy scooter and moped) that I will need to compare to the Segway.*

Washing machine scenario:
- Broad question: Does Major Appliances, Inc. have to honor the extended warranty (give Ms. Ward new washer or $)?
- Preliminary narrow issue: How does the timing of events affect the outcome?
- *Note: To answer the preliminary legal issue, I will need to look at both common law and the U.C.C.*

Independent Practice Exercise 5-1

Execute your research plan for Dr. McMahon's scenario. Record your research using the template suggested in Figure 5-1 or your own template. In order to complete this Exercise, you may need to consult your legal research professor and/or your legal writing professor for assistance.

Independent Practice Exercise 5-2

Execute your research plan for Mr. Clark's scenario. Record your research using the template suggested in Figure 5-1 or your own template. In order to complete this Exercise, you may need to consult your legal research professor and/or your legal writing professor for assistance.

Independent Practice Exercise 5-3

Execute your research plan for Mr. Mordino's scenario. Record your research using the template suggested in Figure 5-1 or your own template. In order to complete this Exercise, you may need to consult your legal research professor and/or your legal writing professor for assistance.

Independent Practice Exercise 5-4

Execute your research plan for Mr. Khan's scenario. Record your research results using the template suggested in Figure 5-1 or your own template. In order to complete this Exercise, you may need to consult your legal research professor and/or your legal writing professor for assistance.

(handwritten margin note, top right)
① Identify which authorities to read carefully
① Mandatory
② possibly helpful

Chapter 6

Reading and Assessing the Relevant Authorities

You have now arrived at a pivotal point in your pre-writing process. Your work in the previous steps has primarily involved gathering information—information about the story, information about your specific assignment, and information about the authorities that are available to help you answer your broad question. You have also taken some steps to organize the information in useful written form.

Now, it is time to begin the important and often demanding work of examining the authorities deeply and critically, to learn specifically what they say, what they mean, and how they relate to the questions you need to answer. Effective legal analysts do not approach this task randomly.

A good first step in the reading process is to identify, based on the skimming you did as you were researching, which authorities you need to read carefully. A practical way to identify these authorities is to review the record of your research and highlight (1) each authority you identified as mandatory and (2) each authority that you categorized as helpful (or possibly helpful). Then you should either create a computer folder of these authorities or print them. *(handwritten margin note: Step 7 in R + A Prep)*

While many of us today default to computer-screen skimming as our preferred method of reading, this default method is almost always insufficient for in-depth legal reading. When you are reading on a computer screen, your ability to move back and forth between parts of statutes, cases, annotations, etc. is severely limited. And you will

Print

> ❶ This does not mean that you should print every authority on your list; be selective. Perhaps begin by printing a few of the most relevant authorities and reading those before deciding to print others. Be especially sensitive to this when statutes and annotations are involved; they can run into the hundreds of pages, so skim them first, and then print the relevant portions.

> ❷ If you have done a good job taking notes on your research, the decision about the order in which to read your authorities should be fairly straightforward. If it is not, you should come to a full stop in your work and consult your research and/or writing professor. You may simply need a refresher on the hierarchy of authority; you may need clarification as to the relationship between the authorities you've found; or you may need to do additional research to find more relevant authorities.

need to do this kind of back-and-forth reading often. Moreover, the distractions that can come your way when you're reading on a computer are almost endless. Because of the limitations of reading screen by screen on the computer, and because you need to avoid distractions as you read, you would be wise to print the authorities you need to read. Then you will easily be able to thumb through them, mark them up, physically arrange and rearrange them, etc.❶

After you have compiled your stack of printed authorities for close reading, you should spend some time thinking about the order in which you will read those authorities. The order may be apparent, especially in situations where there are few authorities. In more complex situations, you should consider the following: Which authorities are mandatory? Of the mandatory authorities, which are most recent? Which cases seem most on point?❷

The reading portion of your pre-writing will be a time-consuming effort that requires complete concentration. You should figure out what steps you need to take to allow for maximum concentration and efficiency. Ask yourself questions such as:

- Where is the best place for me to do my reading? Where will I encounter the fewest distractions? Where will I be comfortable?
- What is the best time for me to do my reading? Am I a morning person? A night owl?
- Am I in the best physical condition to read? Am I hungry? Tired?
- How often do I need to take a break?
- Are there personal issues that need my immediate attention before I can concentrate on my reading?
- Am I trying to multitask while I'm reading?

While there is no "perfect" approach to efficient, concentrated reading, you should be deliberate in creating the reading environment that is most likely to allow you to really, truly concentrate.

6.1 Initial Reading

The first step in your reading should be to read each authority thoroughly *without taking notes*. We refer to this as the "initial reading." This is not the same thing as *skimming* the authorities; at this point you need to read *each word* of each authority, including any footnotes, so that you do not miss something that matters.

There are several reasons for this important initial reading. First, it permits you to take a broad look at the authorities to get a sense of how each one contributes to the resolution of your question and a sense of how the authorities relate to each other. Second, it allows you

Initial Reading

① *allows you to identify + cut authorities*

② *Prevents Premature assessments*

to identify and cull out authorities you thought would be helpful, but turn out not to be, before you've invested significant time in carefully notating them. (If you do cull out any authorities, you should immediately update your research record.) Third, and perhaps most importantly, it prevents you from making premature (and possibly incorrect) assessments about what is and is not important within the authorities.

Reading without taking notes will likely require great self-restraint at first; you may even have to physically put away your pen, highlighter, etc. If you have the self-discipline, you can make limited markings on this initial reading, to remind yourself which portions you think will merit the most attention in your next reading. But if you find yourself giving in to your urge to highlight extensively, make detailed margin notes, etc., put the pen away!

6.2 Close, Active Reading

Close + Active

Once you have taken the step of initially reading each authority from start to finish, you are ready to reread each authority *closely* and *actively*. Your initial reading was a linear reading; now you must read recursively, continuing to circle through the authorities as many times as necessary to locate the "meat" of the authorities.

At this point, you should feel free to move back and forth among the various parts of cases. It may be that your view of the facts will change once you have read the court's holding and reasoning; sometimes a fact that seemed insignificant in your linear reading turns out to be the key fact that determined the court's decision. It may be that the court does not state an explicit rule, thus requiring you to read the various parts of the opinion together to extract an implicit rule. Your goal at this stage of pre-writing is to read closely and actively enough to understand at a deep level how each authority contributes specifically to resolving the questions raised by your assignment.⊙

Close reading requires reading every word of the authority, on the assumption that nothing is in a statute or a case by accident. This close reading can be difficult for beginning law students; they are usually advanced readers who have become skilled at extracting the core ideas from large chunks of text upon a fairly cursory reading. Legal reading is a completely new skill that demands that you slow your eyes down and really focus on the individual words within the authorities.

For example, skipping past a comma can affect your reading and understanding of a sentence. Failing to notice the word "not" can lead to a misunderstanding of an entire paragraph. Brushing past a particular

⊙ Don't be frustrated by the fact that there is no set formula for analyzing the meaning of a case; most of your first year of law school is devoted to learning how to understand court opinions. At this stage, the key skill is recognizing what you do and don't understand about what you're reading and seeking help from professors and, if permitted, from classmates.

fact because it seems uninteresting can lead you to miss the point of the court's reasoning. If you are surprised and frustrated by how long it takes you to read even a short case, that's normal; it probably means that you are doing exactly the kind of close, active reading that is required to allow you to truly understand what you're reading.

Active reading requires more than just paying attention to all of the words; it requires that your mind be *engaged* with the text. You must not just let the words passively enter and exit your brain. You've no doubt had the experience of reading a paragraph and realizing only minutes later that you cannot recall what it said, much less understand what it means. Active reading involves making constant assessments of your own understanding of what you're reading.

There are many strategies that can assist you in reading actively. For example, when reading a case, you might separately mark the key facts, the court's holding, the court's reasoning, the rules that the court used, etc. You might use different colored pens or highlighters to distinguish between the various components of a case or the individual elements of a statute. ❶ You might make margin notes on the printed copy of the case or statute to record your understanding of the key aspects of it. You might circle key terms in a statute, or put a star in the margin beside a key passage in a case. The key is to do whatever helps you stay focused and engaged with the material.

The purpose of reading closely and actively at this stage is two-fold. First, you are seeking to understand what you're reading on a deep level. As stated previously, this will almost always require you to read an authority several times, or to reread certain parts of it, or to read it in a different order, or to flip back and forth between parts of it. Close, active reading is not linear. Second, you are making written notes about key aspects of the authorities that you will return to as you go forward with your pre-writing. If your notes are thorough and reliable, you most likely will not have to spend valuable time later rereading entire cases to complete your assignment. ❷

A few cautions as you begin to read closely and actively: First, don't worry about arriving at "the answer" to your question yet. That will happen in the analysis stage. Be open to being persuaded by different reasoning; for example, you might read one case that leads you to think a Segway *is* "a vehicle such as an automobile," but then the very next case you read might convince you that it *isn't*. That's fine; you don't have to decide yet. The key is that you are actively paying attention to and truly understanding the factual and legal reasons for the different decisions in the two cases and thinking about how they might inform your answer to the questions your client's case raises. ❸

❶ Yes, using different colored highlighters will slow you down as you read; but that is a good thing! However, be careful not to slip into mindless highlighting. Not everything in a case is of equal importance, and not everything is going to be helpful later. If the highlighting isn't helping you stay engaged with the material, then it isn't part of active reading; it's just rote.

❷ If you continue to feel that your efforts to read actively are not leading to a keen understanding of the material you're reading, now is the time to seek out some assistance. Your professor can direct you to helpful resources for addressing this problem.

❸ It's natural for beginning law students to want "the right answer" quickly. But remember, you must learn to embrace the ambiguity of the law. Sometimes there is no absolute right answer to a legal question. Often, the essence of lawyering is determining the better answer to a specific question at a specific point in time based on the specific facts that then exist.

Second, don't read too narrowly. That is, don't immediately reject cases that are not exact matches to your facts, don't exclude cases that seem to suggest an answer you don't like, and don't pay attention only to the parts of the reasoning that seem to support your client's position. You need to keep an open mind, even at the close active reading stage, because you may not yet have found everything you need to allow you to arrive at the "best answer."

Third, don't try to "power through" your close, active reading. This step of the pre-writing process requires you to exercise your metacognitive skills continuously as you move through it. You should pause often to assess how well you understand what you have read. When this self-assessment leads you to realize that you don't understand something, don't just keep going. Stop, reread, consult some outside sources if necessary, spend some time staring out the window and thinking more about what you've read, talk to others or even out loud to yourself—do whatever you have to do to reach a deeper understanding of what you've read.

6.3 Reading and Assessing the Segway Scenario Authorities

The Segway authorities are good vehicles (pun intended) for practicing your close, active reading skills. A review of your research record (see Figure 5-2) reveals that there are three "helpful" or "very helpful" mandatory authorities you need to read carefully: the Graburg red-light statute,[1] the *Shipley* case involving a child's scooter, and the *Monroe* case involving a moped. You note that the two opinions were issued just a couple of months apart; so you would likely decide to read the earlier opinion first, assuming that the later opinion might refer to the earlier one.

You should begin the reading stage of your pre-writing by doing an initial reading of the two opinions in a linear fashion, without making any notes, to get a sense of how each one contributes to the resolution of your question and how the two opinions relate to each other.

Exercise 6-1

Conduct an initial reading of the two fictional opinions that follow.

---

1. Unlike in real life, you can rely on the version of the statute provided in the two cases; in practice you would locate the actual statute in its published form.

872 S.E.2d 278

(Cite as 456 Gr. 123, 872 S.E.2d 278)

Graburg Court of Appeals

Shipley v. State of Graburg

July 17, 2017

Appeal from District Court, Salem County, Jane L. Renfroe, Judge.

Margaret Compton, Assistant State Attorney, for appellant.

Thomas Griffin, Thomas Griffin & Associates, for appellee.

BROWN, Judge.

Traffic ticket on scooter

The defendant in the court below, Janice Shipley, received a traffic ticket when she rode her scooter through a red light. On the morning of April 13, 2016, on the way to mail her income tax forms, the defendant decided she would be able to travel more quickly if she used a two-wheeled scooter, a child's toy that belonged to her young son.

When she approached the intersection of Fourth and Vine in the town of Salem, the traffic light regulating vehicular traffic in her direction of travel was emitting a steady red beam. Because there was no cross traffic, however, the defendant determined that she could cross safely on her scooter.

Stepping up with one leg on the scooter, she pushed off with the other leg and traveled safely through the intersection to the other side of the street and then made her way down the block. Officer Roderick Holmes, sitting in his patrol vehicle, had watched the defendant cross the street. As the defendant was scooting down the block, the officer turned on his siren and attempted to stop the defendant. Because she had not expected to be stopped, she kept going. The police officer stopped at the next corner, stepped from his vehicle, and stopped the defendant from going any further. He then ticketed her for violating Graburg's red-light statute and issued her a warning for resisting arrest.

The defendant pleaded not guilty to the charge of running the red light and filed for dismissal. Her defense was predicated on her belief *defense* that the scooter was not subject to traffic regulations, including the red-light statute. The court below disagreed and found the defendant guilty. The defendant has appealed.

Question before the court →

Therefore, the question before this Court is whether the defendant, traveling on the two-wheeled child's scooter, was subject to the State's traffic laws, including the red-light statute. If the statute did not apply to the defendant, then her failure to stop for the steady red beam was not a violation of the traffic laws, and her case should have been dismissed.

The State's red-light statute reads as follows: "Anyone traveling on or in a vehicle such as an automobile on the public streets shall stop at intersections where a steady red beam of light signals that traffic in the direction being traveled is not allowed. When the beam turns green, the vehicular traveler may proceed." 16 Graburg Gen. Stat. § 2345 (2016). The Graburg Code does not provide a definition of the vehicles to which it applies. Thus, this Court must decide whether a scooter is "a vehicle such as an automobile" that is subject to the statute's other terms.

In the court below, the defendant argued that her two-wheeled scooter was not a "vehicle" subject to the above-referenced statute. The defendant argued that the scooter was not like an automobile, because it was not motorized. Thus, she argued, it should not be subject to the same traffic rules as vehicles with motors. She argued, and the court below agreed, that the purpose of the red-light statute is to protect persons in vehicles traveling through green lights. Thus, the defendant argued that because she was on the two-wheeled scooter, she presented no danger to anyone traveling through the intersection in a motorized vehicle. Therefore, the defendant argued that her scooter was not like an automobile and thus was not subject to the statute.

The State, on the other hand, argued that, because the defendant's scooter had wheels and because she was able, by pushing off, to travel more quickly than she could have on foot, she was subject to the red-light statute even though her scooter had no motor. Therefore, the State argued that the scooter was enough like an automobile to be considered a vehicle and thus subject to the statute even though it had no motor.

We agree with the defendant's argument. While there was no traffic and no one was injured, even if there had been vehicular traffic in the intersection, the defendant's two-wheeled scooter was too light and too slow to have presented a danger to vehicular traffic traveling through the intersection in the direction of the green light. The scooter can move only when pushed by one leg of the operator; thus, it is too slow to be an impediment to crossing vehicular traffic. Further, the scooter is too light in weight to cause anything but cosmetic damage to other vehicles and thus cannot be dangerous enough to be covered by the statute.

Thus, the two-wheeled scooter was not enough like an automobile to be subject to the statute. However, we do not mean to say that every non-motorized conveyance is not subject to the statute. There may well be non-motorized conveyances that are enough like automobiles to fall within the purview of the statute, and we retain our prerogative to so hold.

It is also true that the defendant may have endangered herself through her decision to ignore the red light in her direction, but this appears to be little more than an adult's voluntary and calculated decision. Because we agree that a non-motorized, two-wheeled scooter presents little danger to vehicular traffic, we hold in this case of first impression that dismissal should have been granted by the court below.

Reversed.

NICHOLS, J. and COLLINS, J. concur.

872 S.E.2d 425

(Cite as 456 Gr. 224, 872 S.E.2d 425)

Graburg Court of Appeals

Monroe v. State of Graburg

August 3, 2017

Appeal from District Court, Salem County, Jane L. Renfroe, Judge.

Anne Harmon, Assistant State Attorney, for appellant.

Bruce Thompson for appellee.

PINELLA, Judge.

[handwritten margin note: 1st impression]

[handwritten margin note: decision made by the court]

This Court today decides, for the first time, that drivers of mopeds are subject to the traffic laws of the State of Graburg. We therefore affirm the decision of the trial court below.

[handwritten margin note: deliberate choice]

On April 26, 2016, the defendant, Lefty Monroe, left home to travel to a local club in downtown Salem. He chose to use his moped, because his driver's license had been suspended due to a recent serious driving violation. Because the operators of mopeds are not subject to the same licensing requirements as automobile drivers, the defendant was able to operate his moped legally during the period of his driver's license suspension.

After enjoying refreshments available at the club, the defendant exited to make his way home on his moped. He left the club at midnight. Engaging the motor of the moped, the defendant proceeded on Main Street toward its intersection with Center Avenue. As he approached the intersection on Main Street, the traffic light regulating traffic in his direction of travel turned red. The defendant stopped his moped at the light and put his foot down on the ground to keep from falling. At the same time, the motor on the moped stalled, and, gazing down at the gas gauge, the defendant realized that the moped was out of fuel.

[handwritten margin note: Moped — Traffic violation — Driving while impaired]

Because there were automobiles behind him, the defendant became worried that he would be injured when the light changed to green and he could not move. Therefore, though the light regulating traffic in his direction was still red, the defendant straddled the moped and, after looking both ways to make sure he could move safely through the intersection, maneuvered the moped through the intersection to the other side and off the street.

Officer John Gregory, on patrol on his police motorcycle, was behind the defendant when he pushed his moped through the red light. When the light turned green, Officer Gregory drove across the intersection and over to where the defendant had just stepped off his moped and was standing on the sidewalk. Officer Gregory then proceeded to ticket the defendant for violating the red-light statute and for driving while impaired.

Boardire prom

The defendant, through counsel, moved for dismissal of the red-light charge at the end of the presentation of the State's evidence, which the court denied. In his dismissal motion, the defendant argued that as the driver of a moped, he was not subject to the vehicular laws of the State. In support of his argument, the defendant presented two lines of reasoning.

D's arg

First, the defendant argued that a moped should not be considered a vehicle under Graburg's red-light statute and that, therefore, he had not violated that statute by straddling the moped and maneuvering it through the red light. He based his argument on the fact that, while the moped can use a motor, the motor was not engaged on this occasion and, even if it had been, the moped was capable of traveling only 15 miles per hour at its top rate, thus presenting no danger at all to crossing vehicular traffic. Further, the defendant argued that the moped weighed less than 100 pounds, much less than even the smallest automobile. Relying on another recent decision by this Court, the defendant therefore argued that his moped was not enough "like an automobile" to be subject to the statute, because it was too light and too slow to have endangered motorized traffic in the intersection whether or not the motor was engaged. *See Shipley v. Graburg*, 872 S.E.2d 278, 279 (Graburg Ct. App. 2017) (holding that a scooter was too light and slow to be dangerous to other vehicles and thus was not a vehicle under the statute).

① *Not vehicle*
-speed, weight.

Previous court decision ruling + app

Secondly, the defendant argued that, had the legislature intended for the drivers of mopeds to be subject to vehicular traffic laws, the legislature would not have allowed drivers whose licenses had been suspended to operate mopeds.

② *legislative intent*

The State, on the other hand, argued that all motorized vehicles are enough like automobiles to be considered vehicles and that the driver's licensing matter was immaterial to the issue. The District Court denied the dismissal, and the defendant appealed to this Court.

state arg

The State's red-light statute reads as follows: "Anyone traveling on or in a vehicle such as an automobile on the public streets shall stop at intersections where a steady red beam of light signals that traffic in the direction being traveled is not allowed. When the beam turns green, the vehicular traveler may proceed." 16 Graburg Gen. Stat. § 2345 (2016).

statute

rule

The statute clearly says that the statute requires *anyone* on a vehicle to stop for a red light until the beam becomes green. [Cite omitted.] The defendant surely fits the definition of "anyone." However, it is less clear that the legislature intended the statute to cover *any* vehicle. The only modifier for the word "vehicle" provides the example of an "automobile." [Cite omitted.] Thus, this Court must decide if a moped is a vehicle "such as an automobile" and, therefore, whether the operator of a moped must obey the red-light statute.

issue

While we reserve judgment on whether statutes concerning the licensing of drivers have any connection to the enforcement of traffic laws,

Moped is vehicle
such as automobile
under the statute
① *legislative intent*
② *speed*
③ *weight*

Holding

we do hold that a moped is enough like an automobile to be a "vehicle" under the red-light statute. While it is true that the defendant's moped was not being operated under motor when the defendant passed through the red light, still the moped should be subject to the red-light statute whether the motor was engaged or not. While the presence of the motor alone is not dispositive, surely the legislature intended that a vehicle that could be ridden without any contact with the ground and that was usually self-propelled presented enough danger to crossing traffic and to the driver himself to be subject to the vehicular traffic laws. Further, unlike the scooter in the *Shipley* case, a moped under motor would be able to travel much more quickly than a scooter and is quite a bit heavier than the child's toy referenced in that case.

We therefore agree with the court below and hold that the defendant was subject to the full penalties of the vehicular statutes, and his motion to dismiss was properly denied.

Affirmed.

PARKS, C.J. and SHAPIRO, J. concur.

From this initial linear reading, even without any note-taking, you likely would make some early observations about the two cases:

- One of the vehicles (the moped) qualifies as "a vehicle such as an automobile" under the statute, and the other vehicle (the toy scooter) does not.

- Both cases say the presence of a motor isn't dispositive; what does this mean?

- The main purpose of the statute seems to be to protect other people who are present at the intersection.

- The court in both cases seems to focus on the size, weight, and speed of the vehicle.

If you notice even these few key aspects of the cases, you are doing well with your reading.

Now that you have read the cases thoroughly, taking no notes, you may pick up your pen or highlighter, because now you are going to reread each case *closely* and *actively*, taking careful notes on key aspects of the cases in a form that is helpful to you. Figure 6-1 below is a reprint of the *Shipley* case (the child's scooter case), marked with handwritten notations that highlight important aspects of the case.

Figure 6-1   Hand-Marked Notes on *Shipley* Case

872 S.E.2d 278
(Cite as 456 Gr. 123, 872 S.E.2d 278)

Graburg Court of Appeals

Shipley v. State of Graburg

July 17, 2017 *before Monroe*

Appeal from District Court, Salem County, Jane L. Renfroe, Judge.

Margaret Compton, Assistant State Attorney, for appellant.

Thomas Griffin, Thomas Griffin & Associates, for appellee.

BROWN, Judge.

The defendant in the court below, Janice Shipley received a traffic ticket when she rode her scooter through a red light. On the morning of April 13, 2016, on the way to mail her income tax forms, the defendant decided she would be able to travel more quickly if she used a two-wheeled scooter, a child's toy that belonged to her young son.   *Does it matter why she was on scooter?*

When she approached the intersection of Fourth and Vine in the town of Salem, the traffic light regulating vehicular traffic in her direction of travel was emitting a steady red beam. Because there was no cross traffic, however, the defendant determined that she could cross safely on her scooter.

Stepping up with one leg on the scooter, she pushed off with the other leg and traveled safely through the intersection to the other side of the street and then made her way down the block. Officer Roderick Holmes, sitting in his patrol vehicle, had watched the defendant cross the street. As the defendant was scooting down the block, the officer turned on his siren and attempted to stop the defendant. Because she had not expected to be stopped, she kept going. The police officer stopped at the next corner, stepped from his vehicle, and stopped the defendant from going any further. He then ticketed her for violating Graburg's red-light statute and issued her a warning for resisting arrest.   *Clear violation of statute if scooter is covered*

The defendant pleaded not guilty to the charge of running the red light and filed for dismissal. Her defense was predicated on her belief that the scooter was not subject to traffic regulations, including the red-light statute. The court below disagreed and found the defendant guilty. The defendant has appealed.   *D's arg.*   *D lost at trial court*

Therefore, the question before this Court is whether the defendant, traveling on the two-wheeled child's scooter, was subject to the State's traffic laws, including the red-light statute. If the statute did not apply to the defendant, then her failure to stop for the steady red beam was not a violation of the traffic laws, and her case should have been dismissed.   *ISSUE*

The State's red-light statute reads as follows: "Anyone traveling on or in a vehicle such as an automobile on the public streets shall stop at intersections where a steady red beam of light signals that traffic in the direction being traveled is not allowed. When the beam turns green, the vehicular traveler may proceed." 16 Graburg Gen. Stat. § 2345 (2016). The Graburg Code does not provide a definition of the vehicles to which it applies. Thus, this Court must decide whether a scooter is "a vehicle such as an automobile" that is subject to the statute's other terms.

Narrower issue

In the court below, the defendant argued that her two-wheeled scooter was not a "vehicle" subject to the above-referenced statute. The defendant argued that the scooter was not like an automobile, because it was not motorized. Thus, she argued, it should not be subject to the same traffic rules as vehicles with motors. She argued, and the court below agreed, that the purpose of the red-light statute is to protect persons in vehicles traveling through green lights. Thus, the defendant argued that because she was on the two-wheeled scooter, she presented no danger to anyone traveling through the intersection in a motorized vehicle. Therefore, the defendant argued that her scooter was not like an automobile and thus was not subject to the statute.

Trial ct's reasons for agreeing w/ D's args:
(1) no motor
(2) no danger to others at intersection

The State, on the other hand, argued that, because the defendant's scooter had wheels and because she was able, by pushing off, to travel more quickly than she could have on foot, she was subject to the red-light statute even though her scooter had no motor. Therefore, the State argued that the scooter was enough like an automobile to be considered a vehicle and thus subject to the statute even though it had no motor.

State's args:
(1) quicker than on foot
(2) has wheels
(3) d/n matter if no motor

We agree with the defendant's argument. While there was no traffic and no one was injured, even if there had been vehicular traffic in the intersection, the defendant's two-wheeled scooter was too light and too slow to have presented a danger to vehicular traffic traveling through the intersection in the direction of the green light. The scooter can move only when pushed by one leg of the operator; thus, it is too slow to be an impediment to crossing vehicular traffic. Further, the scooter is too light in weight to cause anything but cosmetic damage to other vehicles and thus cannot be dangerous enough to be covered by the statute.

app. court's reasoning

rule?

Thus, the two-wheeled scooter was not enough like an automobile to be subject to the statute. However, we do not mean to say that every non-motorized conveyance is not subject to the statute. There may well be non-motorized conveyances that are enough like automobiles to fall within the purview of the statute, and we retain our prerogative to so hold.

holding

Ct does not decide motor issue

It is also true that the defendant may have endangered herself through her decision to ignore the red light in her direction, but this appears to be little more than an adult's voluntary and calculated decision. Because we agree that a non-motorized, two-wheeled scooter presents little danger to vehicular traffic, we hold in this case of first impression that dismissal should have been granted by the court below.

dicta?
ct only cares about danger to others

Reversed.

NICHOLS, J. and COLLINS, J. concur.

The marks on the *Shipley* opinion reflect one style of note-taking; your own notes might *look* different. The actual *appearance* of the notes is not important (as long as they're legible and useful to you); what is important is how effectively they capture the key information within the opinion. Moreover, you may not always capture every crucial piece of information during your first close, active reading. If you were to revisit the *Shipley* case after your close, active reading of the *Monroe* case, you would probably notice and mark some additional information.

Exercise 6-2

The *Monroe* opinion is reprinted below. Using whatever technique you prefer, mark up the opinion in a way that emphasizes the key aspects of the *Monroe* case.

872 S.E.2d 425

(Cite as 456 Gr. 224, 872 S.E.2d 425)

Graburg Court of Appeals

Monroe v. State of Graburg

August 3, 2017

Appeal from District Court, Salem County, Jane L. Renfroe, Judge.

Anne Harmon, Assistant State Attorney, for appellant.

Bruce Thompson for appellee.

PINELLA, Judge.

This Court today decides, for the first time, that drivers of mopeds are subject to the traffic laws of the State of Graburg. We therefore affirm the decision of the trial court below.

On April 26, 2016, defendant Lefty Monroe left home to travel to a local club in downtown Salem. He chose to use his moped, because his driver's license had been suspended due to a recent serious driving violation. Because the operators of mopeds are not subject to the same licensing requirements as automobile drivers, the defendant was able to operate his moped legally during the period of his driver's license suspension.

After enjoying refreshments available at the club, the defendant exited to make his way home on his moped. He left the club at midnight. Engaging the motor of the moped, the defendant proceeded on Main Street toward its intersection with Center Avenue. As he approached the intersection on Main Street, the traffic light regulating traffic in his direction of travel turned red. The defendant stopped his moped at the light and put his foot down on the ground to keep from falling. At the same time, the motor on the moped stalled, and, gazing down at the gas gauge, the defendant realized that the moped was out of fuel.

Because there were automobiles behind him, the defendant became worried that he would be injured when the light changed to green and he could not move. Therefore, though the light regulating traffic in his direction was still red, the defendant straddled the moped and, after looking both ways to make sure he could move safely through the intersection, maneuvered the moped through the intersection to the other side and off the street.

Officer John Gregory, on patrol on his police motorcycle, was behind the defendant when he pushed his moped through the red light. When the light turned green, Officer Gregory drove across the intersection and over to where the defendant had just stepped off his moped and was standing on the sidewalk. Officer Gregory then proceeded to ticket the defendant for violating the red-light statute and for driving while impaired.

The defendant, through counsel, moved for dismissal of the red-light charge at the end of the presentation of the State's evidence, which the court denied. In his dismissal motion, the defendant argued that as the driver of a moped, he was not subject to the vehicular laws of the State. In support of his argument, the defendant presented two lines of reasoning.

First, the defendant argued that a moped should not be considered a vehicle under Graburg's red-light statute and that, therefore, he had not violated that statute by straddling the moped and maneuvering it through the red light. He based his argument on the fact that, while the moped can use a motor, the motor was not engaged on this occasion and, even if it had been, the moped was capable of traveling only 15 miles per hour at its top rate, thus presenting no danger at all to crossing vehicular traffic. Further, the defendant argued that the moped weighed less than 100 pounds, much less than even the smallest automobile. Relying on another recent decision by this Court, the defendant therefore argued that his moped was not enough "like an automobile" to be subject to the statute, because it was too light and too slow to have endangered motorized traffic in the intersection whether or not the motor was engaged. *See Shipley v. Graburg*, 872 S.E.2d 278, 279 (Graburg Ct. App. 2017) (holding that a scooter was too light and slow to be dangerous to other vehicles and thus was not a vehicle under the statute).

Secondly, the defendant argued that, had the legislature intended for the drivers of mopeds to be subject to vehicular traffic laws, the legislature would not have allowed drivers whose licenses had been suspended to operate mopeds.

The State, on the other hand, argued that all motorized vehicles are enough like automobiles to be considered vehicles and that the driver's licensing matter was immaterial to the issue. The District Court denied the dismissal, and the defendant appealed to this Court.

The State's red-light statute reads as follows: "Anyone traveling on or in a vehicle such as an automobile on the public streets shall stop at intersections where a steady red beam of light signals that traffic in the direction being traveled is not allowed. When the beam turns green, the vehicular traveler may proceed." 16 Graburg Gen. Stat. § 2345 (2016).

The statute clearly says that the statute requires *anyone* on a vehicle to stop for a red light until the beam becomes green. [Cite omitted.] The defendant surely fits the definition of "anyone." However, it is less clear that the legislature intended the statute to cover *any* vehicle. The only modifier for the word "vehicle" provides the example of an "automobile." [Cite omitted.] Thus, this Court must decide if a moped is a vehicle "such as an automobile" and, therefore, whether the operator of a moped must obey the red-light statute.

While we reserve judgment on whether statutes concerning the licensing of drivers have any connection to the enforcement of traffic laws, we do hold that a moped is enough like an automobile to be a "vehicle" under the red-light statute. While it is true that the defendant's moped was not being operated under motor when the defendant passed through the red light, still the moped should be subject to the red-light statute whether the motor was engaged or not. While the presence of the motor alone is not dispositive, surely the legislature intended that a vehicle that could be ridden without any contact with the ground and that was usually self-propelled presented enough danger to crossing traffic and to the driver himself to be subject to the vehicular traffic laws. Further, unlike the scooter in the *Shipley* case, a moped under motor would be able to travel much more quickly than a scooter and is quite a bit heavier than the child's toy referenced in that case.

We therefore agree with the court below and hold that the defendant was subject to the full penalties of the vehicular statutes, and his motion to dismiss was properly denied.

Affirmed.

PARKS, C.J. and SHAPIRO, J. concur.

Here are some of the aspects of the *Monroe* case that should have stood out to you upon a close, active reading:

- Type of vehicle: moped (motorized).
- Court states at outset that mopeds are covered by red-light stat.
- Motor was not engaged when D ran red light; he pushed moped through intersection.
- D's args: (1) moped's motor was not engaged at time of alleged violation; (2) even if motor had been engaged, moped was too light & too slow to have endangered others at intersection (citing *Shipley* case); (3) if legislature had intended mopeds to be covered, it w/n allow motorists w/suspended licenses to drive mopeds.
- State's args: (1) license issue immaterial; (2) all motorized vehicles are enough like autos to be covered under stat.
- Trial court ruled in favor of State; D appealed.
- Issue: Is moped "vehicle such as auto"? ⓫
- Court's reasoning: any vehicle that can be ridden w/o any contact between driver & ground & is "usually self-propelled" should be covered b/c of danger to operator & others; presence of motor not dispositive & d/n matter that motor wasn't engaged when D ran red light; also, *Shipley* outcome not controlling b/c moped is heavier & can travel faster than child's scooter.

⓫ In your notes, be sure to put quotation marks around the key phrases from the authorities. Then, each time you write those phrases again, retain the quotation marks to remind yourself that those phrases come directly from the authorities themselves.

It is important to understand that, in many instances, you will not be "finished" reading the authorities after your first two readings. You will probably need to revisit each authority several times before you have a complete understanding of how the authorities relate to each other and to your issue (here, whether a Segway is "a vehicle such as an automobile"). How many close, active readings you need to do in any given situation depends partly on the complexity of the authorities and partly on your current experience level as a legal reader. The next exercise is designed to illustrate the importance of rereading each authority as many times as necessary.

Exercise 6-3

Now that you've read and marked up the *Monroe* case, go back and reread the hand-marked *Shipley* case in Figure 6-1. Mark any additional portions of the case that seem important in light of the *Monroe* opinion.

After this second reading of *Shipley*, you might add the following notes to the hand-marked version:

- Operator of child's scooter must make continual repetitive contact w/ground to make scooter move.

- Is scooter "self-propelled"?
- Scooter is child's toy.

In addition, you should be thinking about what facts and reasoning led the court to decide the two cases differently.

This is a good time to pause and consider how far you have come in your understanding of Mr. Byrd's situation. When you first began your pre-writing work, you understood his dilemma in only the most general terms; put another way, you had a layperson's understanding of his situation. You may have initially had a normal emotional reaction to the story: "Gosh, that doesn't seem fair," or "Well, just pay the ticket and get on with life."

However, now you have a lawyer's understanding of the situation. You have moved a long way, from understanding his problem in only the broadest sense toward understanding the specific legal issue that his situation requires you to analyze: Do the characteristics of a Segway, such as its speed, weight, and potential for harm, make it "a vehicle such as an automobile" under the red-light statute? And you have an idea of what you will have to do to answer that question: You'll have to decide how the Segway is like or unlike the toy scooter and the moped discussed in the cases you read. This is significant progress toward fulfilling your commission in Mr. Byrd's case.

6.4 Reading and Assessing the Washing Machine Scenario Authorities

The washing machine scenario illustrates how the reading process works in a different context involving real-life (not fictional) authorities of varying complexity. Recall that in your research results chart for this scenario (see Figure 5-3), you identified the following three authorities as "helpful" or "very helpful":

- S.C. Code Ann. § 36-1-202.
- *Rosenthal v. Walker*, 111 U.S. 185 (1884).
- *White v. Holiday Kamper & Boats*, 2008 WL 4155663.

Again, you should begin your reading process by printing out the three authorities and then considering the logical order in which to read them. Once you have done this, you are ready to begin your initial reading—to read each authority all the way through (you should not just skim) *without taking notes*. Remember your primary goal here: you are seeking to understand in a broad sense how each authority contributes to resolving your narrow issue and how the authorities relate to each other. A secondary goal is to identify the portions of each authority that are irrelevant to your narrow issue, so that in your next reading—your close, active reading—you can focus on only the parts that are directly relevant to answering your question.○

○ After you have done your initial reading of each authority, you might find it helpful to cross out the portions that you are certain you will not need to revisit. Alternatively, you might bracket the portions that seem relevant. Whatever form they take, the purpose of these initial markings, which should be very limited, is to prevent you from focusing on irrelevant portions of the authorities when you turn to your close, active reading.

Exercise 6-4

Print out the three authorities on the above list. Decide on a logical order in which to read them. Then do an initial reading of each authority—that is, read each authority all the way through, without taking notes. You should mark out any portions of the authorities that are irrelevant to your warranty issue, to remind yourself not to focus on them during your later close, active reading.

The washing machine scenario illustrates just how important this initial uncritical reading can be. During your initial reading of the authorities, you probably noticed that portions of them address other aspects of business transactions that are not raised by your client's warranty problem, such as leases, security interests, bills of lading, etc.

For example, the South Carolina commercial code section contains several definitions of terms that are used throughout the code. Of course, not all of these definitions are relevant to the eventual analysis of your narrow issue, but you still need to read all of them once, to identify the definitions that are likely relevant. Likewise, both the Supreme Court case and the South Carolina case contain lengthy discussions of issues and assignments of error that are completely unrelated to your warranty question. However, you would not know this without taking the time to read both cases in their entirety. Spending the time up front reading through the authorities in full will keep you from wasting time later; when you turn to your close, active reading, you will be able to focus on what really matters within each authority.

You likely recognized that it was logical to read the United States Supreme Court case first; it was decided by the highest court in the land, and it dates back to the nineteenth century. Precedent that remains "good law" for that long usually states an important and well-settled rule of law. As your research notes indicate, your interest in this case stems from the fact that it states a rule about mailing versus receipt, which seems directly related to Ms. Ward's question.

Below is an excerpt of the *Rosenthal* case containing the parts of it that you likely identified as relevant to Ms. Ward's case during your initial reading.

111 U.S. 185, 4 S.Ct. 382, 28 L.Ed. 395
Supreme Court of the United States.

ROSENTHAL

v.

WALKER, Assignee, etc.

March 31, 1884.

In Error to the Circuit Court of the United States for the District of Louisiana.

This was an action at law, brought December 30, 1879, by Preston Player, as assignee in bankruptcy of Thomas Carney, against the plaintiff in error, Joseph Rosenthal, under section 5047 of the Revised Statutes, which authorizes an assignee in bankruptcy to recover by suit, in his own name, all the estate, debts, and effects of the bankrupt. The suit was brought to recover from Rosenthal certain money paid and property sold to him by Carney in fraud, as was alleged, of the bankrupt act. A petition in involuntary bankruptcy had been filed against Carney by his creditors October 20, 1875. He was adjudicated a bankrupt March 18, 1876, by the district court for the Eastern District of Missouri, and on May 1, 1876, Player, the defendant in error, was appointed assignee of the estate. The petition, having averred the foregoing facts, alleged that Carney, being insolvent and in contemplation of insolvency, as Rosenthal had reasonable cause to believe, on June 22, 1875, with intent to defeat the operation of the bankrupt law, and to evade its provisions, as Rosenthal well knew, sold and transferred to him 500 cases, containing 50,000 pairs of boots and shoes, of the value of $45,000, and that on July 20th following, to make effectual the fraudulent transfer, Rosenthal agreed that Carney should have an equal interest with him in the goods so sold and transferred, and accordingly recognized and admitted such interest. The petition also averred that Carney, being insolvent and in contemplation of insolvency, as Rosenthal had reasonable cause to believe, and with intent to hinder the operation of the bankrupt law, and evade its provisions, as Rosenthal well knew, on July 22, 1875, sold and transferred to him 100 barrels of whisky, etc., of the value of $9,400, and Carney also stipulated that he should retain an interest in the whisky equal with that of Rosenthal, who then and there recognized said interest accordingly, and that Rosenthal, between July 20, 1875, and March 1, 1876, disposed of and converted to his own use all the property so sold and transferred to him.

The petition further alleged that Carney, between July 20 and August 23, 1875, inclusive, being insolvent and in contemplation of insolvency, as Rosenthal had reasonable cause to believe, and with the purpose of defeating the object and hindering the operation of the bankrupt law, as Rosenthal well knew, made to him certain payments of money, amounting in the aggregate to $30,000. The petition then made the following averment: 'The plaintiff states that both the said Carney and the defendant kept concealed from him, the said plaintiff, the fact of the said payment and transfer of the said aggregate sum of $30,000, hereinbefore mentioned, and of all the component parts thereof; and also kept concealed from him the fact of the sale, transfer, and conveyance of the said goods and merchandise hereinafter set forth, and that he, the said plaintiff, did not obtain knowledge and information of the said matters, or either of them, until the twenty-ninth day of November, 1879, and then for the first time the said matters were disclosed to him and brought to his knowledge.'

Rosenthal excepted to the petition on two grounds,- *First*, because, as appeared on its face, the suit was not brought within two years from the time when the cause of action accrued; and, *second*, because the said sale of boots and shoes, alleged to have been made by Carney to Rosenthal on June 22, 1875, was not made within three months next before the filing of the petition in bankruptcy against Carney. The court overruled the first exception absolutely, and ordered that the second exception 'be dismissed so as not to prejudice the right of plaintiff to prove any of the transactions alleged in said petition to have taken place on the twentieth day of July, 1875, and within three months next before the institutions of proceedings in bankruptcy against the bankrupt, Thomas Carney, and maintaining said ground of exception only so far as relates to the transfer and sale of five hundred cases of boots and shoes, alleged to have been made on the twenty-second day of June, 1875. But the plaintiff shall have the right to prove, as by him alleged, that subsequently to June 22, 1875, the bankrupt, by agreement with defendant, was reinvested with an interest in said goods, and thereafter, within three months, the goods were disposed of as alleged.'

On March 3, 1880, Rosenthal filed his answer, which was a general denial of all the averments of the petition. On December 7th following, after the trial had commenced, he filed the following plea and supplemental answer: 'Now comes the defendant and pleads the prescription of two years, as provided for in the bankruptcy act, sec. 5057, of the Revised Statutes of the United States, in bar of plaintiff's action. And for supplemental answer to petition of plaintiff, defendant specially denies that the matters and things alleged in plaintiff's petition were first disclosed to him on November 29, 1879, as alleged; but avers that said plaintiff had full knowledge of all transactions that ever took place between the defendant and Carney, bankrupt, at the time said plaintiff was elected assignee.' On the motion of the plaintiff the supplemental answer was stricken out, and the defendant excepted, but, as the record shows, 'during the trial of the cause no restraint was put upon the defendant in offering evidence as to the knowledge of plaintiff, as alleged in that part of the supplemental answer which was stricken out, and both sides offered evidence as to such knowledge, and the court, upon this point, left it to the jury to say whether the action was commenced within two years from the time when the plaintiff knew, or by due diligence might have known, of the cause of action.' The pleadings having been thus made up, the issues of fact were submitted to a jury, which returned a verdict for the plaintiff for $17,500, on which the court rendered judgment against the defendant. To reverse that judgment this writ of error is prosecuted. Player, the original assignee, having died after the judgment in the circuit court, W. R. Walker was appointed assignee and substituted as defendant in error in his stead.

[Discussion of first two assignments of error omitted]

The next assignment of error relates to the admission in evidence by the circuit court of certain letter-press copies of letters written by Carney to the plaintiff in error. The record shows that Carney testified that, while he was in St. Louis and the plaintiff in error in New Orleans, they were corresponding with each other; that several letters were written by each to the other, and were received by each from the other; that Carney, having so testified, produced two letters purporting to have been addressed by the plaintiff in error, in New Orleans, to him at St. Louis, and which he testified he had received through the mails. These letters having been admitted in evidence, Carney produced certain letter-press copies of letters which he testified he had written to the plaintiff in error, and mailed with his own hand in the post office at St. Louis, postage prepaid, directed to the plaintiff in error at New Orleans, and to his proper address in that city. The record also shows that in response to a *subpoena duces tecum* the plaintiff in error swore that he never received the letters addressed to him by Carney. Upon this state of the evidence, the defendant in error offered to read to the jury the letterpress copies of the letters which Carney swore he had mailed to the plaintiff in error. They were objected to, but were admitted by the court in spite of the objection. This action of the court is now urged as a ground for reversing the judgment.

We think the copies were properly admitted in evidence. The point in dispute between the parties was whether the original letters had been received by the plaintiff in error. One of the letters from the plaintiff in error to Carney is clearly in answer to two of the letters which Carney swears he mailed to him, and is proof that those letters were received by him. Independently of this fact, the proof that the letters were received by the plaintiff in error was *prima facie* sufficient, and the court properly allowed the copies to go to the jury, leaving them to decide, on all the evidence, whether the originals had been received. The rule is well settled that if a letter properly directed is proved to have been either put into the post-office or delivered to the postman, it is presumed, from the known course of business in the post-office department, that it reached its destination at the regular time, and was received by the person to whom it was addressed. *Saunderson* v. *Judge*, 2 H. Bl. 509; *Woodcock* v. *Houldsworth*, 16 Mees. & W. 124; *Dunlop* v. *Higgins*, 1 H. L. Cas. 381; *Callan* v. *Gaylord*, 3 Watts, 321; *Starr* v. *Torrey*, 2 Zab. 190; *Tanner* v. *Hughes*, 53 Pa. St. 289; *Howard* v. *Daly*, 61 N. Y. 362; *Huntley* v. *Whittier*, 105 Mass. 392. As was said by GRAY, J., in the case last cited, 'the presumption so arising is not a conclusive presumption of law, but a mere inference of fact, founded on the probability that the officers of the government will do their duty and the usual course of business; and, when it is opposed by evidence that the letters never were received, must be weighed with all the other circumstances of the case, by the jury in determining the question whether the letters were actually received or not.' The presumption that a letter was received is based on considerations that it is perfectly clear that it applies without regard to the contents of the letter. The contention, therefore, of counsel for plaintiff in error that the presumption fails when the contents of the letter would, if the letter were received, tend to subject the party receiving it to a penalty or forfeiture, is not well founded. The rule and the authorities cited in support of it sustain the action of the court in admitting in evidence the copies of the letters, and in submitting to the jury the question whether the letters had been received, to be decided upon all the testimony bearing upon the point.

[Discussion of final assignment of error omitted]

There are other assignments of error which have not been argued by the counsel for the plaintiff in error. Most of them have been covered by what we have said. The others present, in our opinion, no good ground for the reversal of the judgment. We find no error in the record. The judgment of the circuit court is therefore affirmed.

Note that this excerpt contains the Court's entire, lengthy recitation of the facts of the case and its procedural history. You must capture the "whole story," wherever its parts appear within the opinion. Even if parts of the story seem unrelated to your client's question, they are nonetheless important at this stage of your pre-writing. After you do your close, active reading, you can then decide which facts were key to the Court's reasoning, and those facts will be the basis for your later analysis of your question. As for the procedural history, it is always important, because it provides the context for a court's consideration of the issues discussed in the opinion.

The above excerpt omits the portions of the opinion that discuss assignments of error unrelated to the rule about mailing versus receipt. (Of course, you would not know that they are unrelated unless you had read the entire opinion in full.) Thus, the excerpt contains only the portions of the opinion that are relevant to Ms. Ward's question.

Perhaps you chose to read the South Carolina code section next; it makes perfect sense to read the code section itself before you read the *White* case that references it.❍ After your initial reading, you likely identified the definitions in subsections (d) and (e) as the ones that will require close, active reading.

Subsections (d) and (e) read as follows:

❍ If you chose to read the case first, this isn't fatal. The key is that you carefully read both authorities in an order that makes logical sense to your pre-writing process. You should be able to articulate your logic: "I chose to read the *White* case first because…."

Code of Laws of South Carolina 1976 Annotated
Title 36. Commercial Code
Chapter 1. Commercial Code—General Provisions
Part 2. General Definitions and Principles of Interpretation

§ 36-1-202. Notice; knowledge.

(d) A person "notifies" or "gives" a notice or notification to another person by taking such steps as may be reasonably required to inform the other person in ordinary course, whether or not the other person actually comes to know of it.

(e) Subject to subsection (f), a person "receives" a notice or notification when:

  (1) it comes to that person's attention; or

  (2) it is duly delivered in a form reasonable under the circumstances at the place of business through which the contract was made or at another location held out by that person as the place for receipt of such communications.

The final authority on the list is the *White* case. Based on your initial reading, you likely identified the portions printed below as worthy of close, active reading.

United States District Court,
D. South Carolina,
Spartanburg Division.

Bevis WHITE and Georgia White, Plaintiffs,
v.
HOLIDAY KAMPER & BOATS, Fleetwood Enterprises, Inc., and Bank of the West, Defendants.

Civil Action No. 7:06-02362-HFF.
Sept. 9, 2008.

MEMORANDUM OPINION AND ORDER GRANTING IN PART AND DENYING IN PART DEFENDANTS' MOTION FOR PARTIAL SUMMARY JUDGMENT

HENRY F. FLOYD, District Judge.

I. INTRODUCTION

This is a breach of warranty action. Pending before the Court is Defendants' motion for partial summary judgment as to the following issues: (1) breach of implied warranty of fitness for particular purpose as to all Defendants, (2) revocation of acceptance as to all Defendants, (3) the common law tort claim of negligence and/or negligent misrepresentation as to all Defendants, and (4) violations of the Magnuson-Moss Warranty Act (the Act) as to Defendant Fleetwood Motor Homes of Indiana, Inc. (Defendant Fleetwood). The Court has jurisdiction over this matter pursuant to 28 U.S.C. §§ 1331 and 1367. Having carefully considered the motion, the response, the reply, the record, and the applicable law, it is the judgment of this Court that Defendants' motion for partial summary judgment be granted as to Plaintiff's claims of (1) breach of implied warranty of fitness for particular purpose as to all Defendants; (2) revocation of acceptance as to all Defendants; and (3) the common law tort claim of negligence and/or negligent misrepresentation as to all Defendants, and denied as to Plaintiff's claims of violations of the Act.

II. FACTUAL AND PROCEDURAL HISTORY

The Court will construe the facts in the light most favorable to Plaintiffs.

Plaintiffs, who live outside of Knoxville, Tennessee, purchased a 2005 Fleetwood Revolution RV from Defendant Holiday Kamper & Boats (Defendant Holiday Kamper) on May 19, 2005, for the purchase price of $226,506.00. Defendant Bank of the West (Defendant Bank) is the assignee of the retail installment sales contract originated by Defendant Holiday Kamper. Defendant Fleetwood is the manufacturer of the RV and provided a written warranty for Plaintiffs' RV.

At the time of purchase, the mileage of the RV was 1,500 miles. Upon delivery, Plaintiffs experienced continuing problems with the RV. Over the next year, Plaintiffs made repeated attempts to repair the various defects, but contend that certain problems have not been resolved. In addition, Plaintiff Bevis White telephoned Defendant Fleetwood to alert them to the defects with the RV. On three separate occasions, Bevis White spoke with a Defendant Fleetwood representative and on all three occasions he did not receive the requested assistance.

On April 13, 2006, Plaintiffs took the RV to Defendant Holiday Kamper for its last known repair. Technicians noted that the RV had been driven approximately 5,950 miles. During repair, Plaintiffs state that they verbally communicated their desire for revocation of sale to Defendant Holiday Kamper. Specifically, Plaintiffs maintain that they told Defendant Holiday Kamper's management that they wanted a refund. In addition, on May 1, 2006, Plaintiffs' counsel mailed Defendant Fleetwood written notice concerning Plaintiff's alleged revocation, Defendants' continuing breach of warranty and their failure to repair. Plaintiffs' counsel mailed the notice to the address provided by Defendant Fleetwood in the warranty booklet that accompanies each RV. Although the RV was still under warranty, neither Defendant Fleetwood nor Defendant Holiday Kamper responded.

Plaintiffs subsequently filed suit against Defendants on June 28, 2006. Defendants removed the action to this Court on August 24, 2006.

In December 2007, the mileage of the RV was an estimated 11,000 miles, approximately 5,000 miles more than on April 13, 2006, the date Plaintiffs allegedly demanded revocation of acceptance. Since the purported revocation, Plaintiffs have lived in the RV for a period of time between selling and purchasing a new home in Tennessee, taken five or six trips to their daughter's home in Atlanta, Georgia, and driven to Jacksonville, Florida for a three-week trip. Further, since the beginning of the case at bar, Plaintiffs have taken a trip to Jacksonville, Florida, and then back through Atlanta, Georgia, that, in whole, lasted over one month.

III. STANDARD OF REVIEW

Rule 56(c) of the Federal Rules of Civil Procedure provides that summary judgment "shall be rendered forthwith if the pleadings, depositions, answers to interrogatories and admissions on file, together with affidavits, if any, show that there is no genuine issue as to any material fact and that the moving party is entitled to a judgment as a matter of law." The moving party bears this initial burden of informing the Court of the basis for its motions, and identifying those portions of the record "which it believes demonstrate the absence of a genuine issue of material fact." *Celotex Corp. v. Catrett,* 477 U.S. 317, 323, 106 S.Ct. 2548, 91 L.Ed.2d 265 (1986). The Court reviews the record by drawing all inferences most favorable to the party opposing the motion. *Matsushita Elec. Indus. Co. v. Zenith Radio Corp.,* 475 U.S. 574, 587, 106 S.Ct. 1348, 89 L.Ed.2d 538 (1986) (citing *United States v. Diebold, Inc.,* 369 U.S. 654, 82 S.Ct. 993, 8 L.Ed.2d 176 (1962)).

"Once the moving party carries its burden, the adverse party may not rest upon the mere allegations or denials of the adverse party's pleadings, but the adverse party's response ... must set forth specific facts showing that there is a genuine issue for trial." Fed.R.Civ.P. 56(e). The adverse party must show more than "some metaphysical doubt as to the material facts." *Matsushita,* 475 U.S. at 586. If an adverse party completely fails to make an offer of proof concerning an essential element of that party's case on which that party will bear the burden of proof, then all other facts are necessarily rendered immaterial and the moving party is entitled to summary judgment. *Celotex,* 477 U.S. at 322-23. Hence, the granting of summary judgment involves a three-tier analysis. First, the Court determines whether a genuine issue actually exists so as to necessitate a trial. Fed.R.Civ.P. 56(e). An issue is genuine "if the evidence is such that a reasonable [trier of fact] could return a verdict for the nonmoving party." *Anderson v. Liberty Lobby, Inc.,* 477 U.S. 242, 248, 106 S.Ct. 2505, 91 L.Ed.2d 202 (1986). Second, the Court must ascertain whether that genuine issue pertains to material facts. Fed.R.Civ.P. 56(e). The substantial law of the case identifies the material facts, that is, those facts that potentially affect the outcome of the suit. *Anderson,* 477 U.S. at 248. Third, assuming no genuine issue exists as to the material facts, the Court will decide whether the moving party shall prevail solely as a matter of law. Fed.R.Civ.P. 56(e).

Summary judgment is "properly regarded not as a disfavored procedural shortcut, but rather as an integral part of the Federal Rules as a whole, which are designed to secure the just, speedy and inexpensive determination of every action." *Celotex,* 477 U.S. at 327. The primary issue is whether the material facts present a sufficient disagreement as to require a trial, or whether the facts are sufficiently one-sided that one party should prevail as a matter of law. *Anderson,* 477 U.S. at 251-52. The substantive law of the case identifies which facts are material. *Id.* at 248. Only disputed facts potentially affecting the outcome of the suit under the substantive law preclude the entry of summary judgment.

[Part IV, Contentions of the Parties, is omitted.] ⓘ

V. DISCUSSION AND ANALYSIS

[Sections A, B, and C of Part V are omitted.] ⓘ

D. "Reasonable opportunity to cure" the "failure to comply" under the Act

The Act, 15 U.S.C. § 2310, was enacted by Congress in response to the widespread misuse by merchants of express warranties and disclaimers. 15 U.S.C.A. § 2401. The Act "operates in conjunction with state law to regulate the warranting of consumer products." *Carlson v. General Motors Corp.,* 883 F.2d 287, 291 (4th Cir.1989). "Congress intended the application of state law, except as expressly modified by [the Act], in ... breach of warranty actions." *Walsh v. Ford Motor Co.,* 807 F.2d 1000, 1012 (D.C.Cir.1986) (stating that the Act was intended to supplement, not supplant, state law.) Therefore, inasmuch as the Act does not modify [South Carolina] law, the UCC of South Carolina is the proper authority. *See Carlson,* 883 F.2d at 291-92 (applying S.C. Code Ann. § 36-2-101 in conjunction with the Act.)

The Act is aimed at written warranties and service contracts made in connection with the sale of "consumer products." 15 U.S.C. § 2301(1). Specifically, it provides that for a warrantor to meet the federal minimum standards for warranty, the warrantor must remedy the consumer product within a reasonable time and without charge. *Id.*

To bring a cause of action under the Act, the party in non-compliance with the contract must be notified and given a "reasonable opportunity to cure" the "failure to comply." 15 U.S.C. § 2310(e). The South Carolina UCC provides that "[a] person 'receives' a notice or notification when it is duly delivered in a form reasonable under the circumstances at the place of business through which the contract was made or at another location held out by that person as the place for receipt of such communications." S.C. Code Ann. § 36-1-201. ⓘ Alternatively, "[a] person 'notifies' or 'gives' a notice or notification to another person by taking such steps as may be reasonably required to inform the other person in ordinary course, whether or not the other person actually comes to know of it." *Id.*

In this case, Plaintiff Bevis White maintains that he telephoned Defendant Fleetwood three times. Moreover, Plaintiffs' counsel mailed notice to the address given in the warranty booklet provided by Defendant Fleetwood. Defendant Fleetwood, however, contends that it never received notification. Nevertheless, Plaintiffs' duty to notify ends once

ⓘ In your initial reading, you likely recognized that most of this section relates to issues that have nothing to do with Ms. Ward's situation, and you may have marked through them to remind yourself not to focus on them during your close, active reading.

ⓘ In your initial reading, you likely recognized that reading these lengthy sections of the opinion would be a waste of your time, because they are not relevant to Ms. Ward's situation. As a busy law student (or a busy lawyer), your time is too precious to spend on a close, active reading of irrelevant material.

ⓘ The relevant code section was renumbered in October 2014 as part of a series of amendments to the code. While the *White* case cites § 36-1-201, the quoted language is identical to the current language of section § 36-1-202 that appears on page 84.

they have "tak[en] such steps as may be reasonably required to inform" Defendant Fleetwood of their duty to comply with the warranty. *See* S.C. Code Ann. § 36-1-202(d).

Moreover, Plaintiffs waited from May 1, 2007, to June 28, 2007, (almost two months) before commencing this action in state court. During that two month period, Defendant Fleetwood, nor any of the other Defendants, contacted Plaintiffs in an attempt to comply with the extended warranty. Hence, inasmuch as Plaintiffs allowed Defendant Fleetwood a "reasonable opportunity to cure" their "failure to comply," *See* 15 U.S.C. § 2310(e), Plaintiffs' claim pursuant to the Act will survive Defendants' motion for summary judgment.

VI. CONCLUSION

Based on the foregoing discussion and analysis, it is the judgment of this Court that Defendants' motion for partial summary judgment is hereby **GRANTED** as to Plaintiff s claims of (1) breach of implied warranty of fitness for particular purpose as to all Defendants; (2) revocation of acceptance as to all Defendants; and (3) the common law tort claim of negligence and/or negligent misrepresentation as to all Defendants, and **DENIED** as to Plaintiff's claims of violations of the Act.

IT IS SO ORDERED.

The excerpt above includes the Introduction and the Factual and Procedural Background sections, for the same reasons that they were included in the *Rosenthal* excerpt. The Standard of Review section is also included, because the standard of review is always important to your understanding of the context of the case.[2]

Only the final portion of the Discussion section is included in the excerpt. After your initial reading of the case, you likely recognized that the first three portions of the Discussion decide issues unrelated to Ms. Ward's question.

Having whittled down the authorities to the portions relevant to Ms. Ward's warranty claim, you are ready to move to the close, active reading step of your pre-writing process. Although the washing machine authorities are very different from the ones you read in the Segway scenario, your goal here is the same: to gain a deep understanding of what the authorities say and how they help you resolve Ms. Ward's question.

Turning to the *Rosenthal* case, you would begin your close, active reading by poring through the case to get a clear picture of what happened factually in the case—that is, to understand "the story." This may take more time than you expect; unlike the cases in the Segway scenario, which are factually straightforward, the story in *Rosenthal* is more complex. In addition, the language of the opinion is antiquated, making it harder to understand. The wordy style of communication used in 1884 bears little resemblance to the stripped-down language you may be used to reading in e-mails, texts, and tweets. ❶ It may feel like torture to tease out the key facts of these older cases, but you must discipline yourself to do it.

As you begin reading, you will immediately recognize the need to spend a little bit of time sorting through the "cast of characters" in the story. This is often necessary in older cases that use obsolete terminology in referring to the parties. It would be a waste of your time to continue reading through any case without having a clear picture of who the parties are: Who sued whom in the trial court? Who won at the trial level? Who is bringing the appeal?

❶ Note that the first full paragraph of the opinion, reprinted on page 80, is very long but contains just six sentences; two of them span more than nine lines each. This presents a major impediment to your comprehension of the case, but if you go slowly, phrase by phrase, you will eventually figure out what the Court is saying. Fortunately, courts today tend to write opinions in a much more readable style.

---

2. The standard of review in the trial court determines the scope of the court's consideration of the facts and the law. In the *White* case, for example, the discussion of the summary judgment standard tells you how the court will construe the key facts (in the light most favorable to the plaintiffs). This simply provides additional context for you as you closely and actively read the opinion. Although standards of review are usually not heavily emphasized in first-year law school courses, you should not ignore them in your close, active reading. If you do not understand the standard of review in any given opinion, you should take steps to remedy that before you continue closely and actively reading the rest of the opinion.

One good way to clarify the "cast of characters" in this case, or any case, is to make a list of the parties *by name* and identify their roles in the story. You may have to read the case several times to be able to untangle the relationships among the parties, and you may need to consult a legal dictionary if the opinion uses unfamiliar or antiquated terms. Avoid using legal terminology such as "plaintiff in error" or "assignee in bankruptcy." A close reading of the first three paragraphs of the *Rosenthal* opinion might result in the list shown below in Figure 6-2:

Figure 6-2 List of Parties in *Rosenthal* and Their Roles in the Case

---

- Carney: person whose actions (fraudulent transfers of property to Rosenthal) led to lawsuit.
- Player: original plaintiff; representative of Carney's creditors who was trying to get the value of the fraudulent transfers back from Rosenthal so that Carney's creditors could get paid.
- Rosenthal: original defendant to whom Carney allegedly made fraudulent transfers of property to avoid paying his creditors.
- Walker: took Player's place upon Player's death; no real role in the story.

Now that you understand who is who, you can reframe the story as you continue to read, substituting names for legal terms. For example, every time you see the term "plaintiff in error" (an antiquated term for the losing party at trial; today we would use the term "appellant"), you should substitute the actual name "Rosenthal." In your early efforts at reading cases, you may even want to do this in writing—for example, every time you see "plaintiff in error," cross it out and write "Rosenthal" instead.

This reframing will help you understand what facts gave rise to the dispute between the parties and how the trial court resolved the dispute. In essence, the *Rosenthal* case is about two men—Carney and Rosenthal—who allegedly conspired to defraud Carney's creditors. When Player, a representative of the creditors, sued Rosenthal to recover the fraudulently transferred property, Rosenthal claimed that he did not know that Carney was in bankruptcy and that he did not realize the transfers Carney made to him were fraudulent. Carney, however, claimed that Rosenthal was a willing participant in the fraudulent transfers and that the two had an agreement to split whatever property they successfully concealed from Carney's creditors. The trial court admitted certain letters written from Carney to Rosenthal as evidence of Rosenthal's collusion in Carney's scheme.

Based in part on these letters, the jury found in favor of Carney's creditors, and the trial court entered judgment against Rosenthal. Rosenthal then appealed.

Do not be discouraged if you did not fully understand the story upon your first close, active reading. In fact, it would likely take several readings of this opinion to arrive at a complete understanding of the story. You should read an opinion as many times as necessary to boil it down to the key information you will need to understand the reasoning in the portion of the opinion that bears directly on the legal question you are seeking to answer. The above summary of *Rosenthal*, for example, confirms your initial impression that only a small part of the opinion is relevant to your analysis of Ms. Ward's warranty dispute with Major Appliances, Inc.—the part that discusses Carney's claim that he mailed the letters to Rosenthal and Rosenthal's claim that he never received them.

At this point, you want to turn your attention to that small part of the opinion, making careful notations about the rules and reasoning the Court used to arrive at its decision that the letters were properly admitted into evidence. In this instance, making a bulleted list like the ones you created for the Segway cases might work, but you should consider other approaches as well.❶ Because the *Rosenthal* case is written in antiquated language, a more helpful technique than bulleting might be paraphrasing the Court's discussion using simple, modern terms. You might even write out your paraphrase; this written paraphrase will not only aid your understanding, but will also be helpful later when you must explain your analysis of Ms. Ward's situation to Attorney Cox and to Ms. Ward herself.❷

❶ A case brief would also work, if it is detailed enough to capture the critical information.

As you work through the next few exercises, remember that they are designed to give you practice in reading closely and actively—a skill that is essential to the work that lawyers do every day. While the results of your work on these exercises will be specific to the legal question presented by the washing machine scenario, the techniques you use will be transferable to any legal analysis you are asked to undertake.

❷ Whatever notation technique you use, your goal is to capture in usable form the facts and law from the case that you will later need to return to in the analysis stage of your pre-writing; you do not want to have to stop during your analysis and reread entire cases. Thus, before moving on to the analysis step, take a few minutes to consider whether you fully understand the authorities. If not, don't go forward. A good test of your level of understanding is to ask yourself whether you could clearly explain the cases to a classmate who has not read them.

Exercise 6-5

Below are the two paragraphs of *Rosenthal* that contain the Court's discussion of the alleged mailing and receipt of the letters from Carney to Rosenthal. Write out a simple, modern paraphrase of these two paragraphs:

The next assignment of error relates to the admission in evidence by the circuit court of certain letter-press copies of letters written by Carney to the plaintiff in error. The record shows that Carney testified that, while he was in St. Louis and the plaintiff in error in New Orleans, they were corresponding with each other; that several letters were written by each to the other, and were received by each from the other; that Carney, having so testified, produced two letters purporting to have been addressed by the plaintiff in error, in New Orleans, to him at St. Louis, and which he testified he had received through the mails. These letters having been admitted in evidence, Carney produced certain letter-press copies of letters which he testified he had written to the plaintiff in error, and mailed with his own hand in the post office at St. Louis, postage prepaid, directed to the plaintiff in error at New Orleans, and to his proper address in that city. The record also shows that in response to a *subpoena duces tecum* the plaintiff in error swore that he never received the letters addressed to him by Carney. Upon this state of the evidence, the defendant in error offered to read to the jury the letterpress copies of the letters which Carney swore he had mailed to the plaintiff in error. They were objected to, but were admitted by the court in spite of the objection. This action of the court is now urged as a ground for reversing the judgment.

We think the copies were properly admitted in evidence. The point in dispute between the parties was whether the original letters had been received by the plaintiff in error. One of the letters from the plaintiff in error to Carney is clearly in answer to two of the letters which Carney swears he mailed to him, and is proof that those letters were received by him. Independently of this fact, the proof that the letters were received by the plaintiff in error was *prima facie* sufficient, and the court properly allowed the copies to go to the jury, leaving them to decide, on all the evidence, whether the originals had been received. The rule is well settled that if a letter properly directed is proved to have been either put into the post-office or delivered to the postman, it is presumed, from the known course of business in the post-office department, that it reached its destination at the regular time, and was received by the person to whom it was addressed. *Saunderson* v. *Judge*, 2 H. Bl. 509; *Woodcock* v. *Houldsworth*, 16 Mees. & W. 124; *Dunlop* v. *Higgins*, 1 H. L. Cas. 381; *Callan* v. *Gaylord*, 3 Watts, 321; *Starr* v. *Torrey*, 2 Zab. 190; *Tanner* v. *Hughes*, 53 Pa. St. 289; *Howard* v. *Daly*, 61 N. Y. 362; *Huntley* v. *Whittier*, 105 Mass. 392. As was said by GRAY, J., in the case last cited, 'the presumption so arising is not a conclusive presumption of law, but a mere inference of fact, founded on the probability that the officers of the government will do their duty and the usual course of business; and, when it is opposed by evidence that the letters never were received, must be weighed with all the other circumstances of the case, by the jury in determining the question whether the letters were actually received or not.' The presumption that a letter was received is based on considerations that it is perfectly clear that it applies without regard to the contents of the let-

ter. The contention, therefore, of counsel for plaintiff in error that
the presumption fails when the contents of the letter would, if the
letter were received, tend to subject the party receiving it to a
penalty or forfeiture, is not well founded. The rule and the authorities cited in support of it sustain the action of the court in admitting
in evidence the copies of the letters, and in submitting to the jury
the question whether the letters had been received, to be decided
upon all the testimony bearing upon the point.

Now, check your paraphrase against the sample paraphrase below:

Figure 6-3 Sample Paraphrase of Key Portion of *Rosenthal*

Rosenthal challenged the trial court's admission of copies of letters
allegedly written to him by Carney and mailed to him by Carney himself.
Carney produced copies of these letters, which he said that he hand-
wrote and personally mailed at the post office in St. Louis (with proper
postage) to Rosenthal at his proper address in New Orleans. Rosenthal
swore in court that he never received the letters. Carney was allowed to
read these letters into evidence over Rosenthal's objection.

The Supreme Court held that the letters were properly admitted. For
one thing, Carney produced a letter he had received from Rosenthal that
was in direct response to one of the letters Carney said he mailed to
Rosenthal; this was proof that Rosenthal received that letter. Even if that
had not been proven, there is a well-settled rule that creates a presumption that Rosenthal received the letters from Carney: "If a letter properly
directed [addressed] is proved to have been either put into the post-office
or delivered to the postman, it is presumed, from the known course of
business in the post-office department, that it reached its destination at
the regular time, and was received by the person to whom it was addressed." However, the jury will still weigh all the evidence to decide
whether the letters were actually received or not. In this case, the
Supreme Court held that there was no basis for reversing the trial court's
decision to admit the letters into evidence.

Note that the above paraphrase quotes the Court's own language
for the rule that will apply to Ms. Ward's situation. When paraphrasing
parts of judicial opinions, you should be careful to retain key language
verbatim; you do not want to risk misstating the applicable rules. In
this instance, it is easy to know which language to quote, because the
Court says, "The rule is well-settled that...." In many opinions, the
rule is not explicitly identified; in fact, it is often necessary to construct
the rule from different pieces of the court's opinion. Whatever the
source of the governing rule, you should generally avoid paraphrasing
any language that seems to be part of it.

○ The word "presumed" in this context is a legal "term of art"—a familiar word that has a specific legal meaning. You should maintain a healthy curiosity about the words courts use; it is never wrong to look up a term, even one that seems familiar, to gain a deeper understanding of its legal meaning. In fact, it is your responsibility to constantly question what you read to make sure that you really understand what it means. In this scenario, because the case itself uses the term "presumed," you need to be certain, before you continue with your pre-writing process, that you understand the legal meaning of "presumed."

\
Elements

Whether or not they received notice under the warranty

After reading *Rosenthal* closely and actively, you now have a good understanding of the common-law rule[3] that applies to Ms. Ward's situation:

> **When a letter is properly addressed and properly deposited in the mail, it is presumed○ that the letter was received by the addressee in the known course of business.**

This rule serves as a sort of "baseline"—a starting point from which you will move forward to the other authorities. As you move to your close, active reading of the South Carolina statute and the *White* case, you should be asking yourself how those authorities interact with the "baseline" rule from *Rosenthal*.

As you determined previously, the next authority to read closely and actively is the South Carolina statute, S.C. Code Ann. § 36-1-202. Recall that your initial reading led you to focus on subsections (d) and (e), which are reprinted below.

Code of Laws of South Carolina 1976 Annotated
Title 36. Commercial Code
Chapter 1. Commercial Code—General Provisions
Part 2. General Definitions and Principles of Interpretation

§ 36-1-202. Notice; knowledge.

(d) A person "notifies" or "gives" a notice or notification to another person by taking such steps as may be reasonably required to inform the other person in ordinary course, whether or not the other person actually comes to know of it.

→ (e) Subject to subsection (f), a person "receives" a notice or notification when:

  (1) it comes to that person's attention; or

  (2) it is duly delivered at the place of business through which the contract was made or at any other place held out by that person as the place for receipt of such communications.

You will probably notice that your close, active reading of this statute is a more straightforward task than your close, active reading of *Rosenthal*. As a rule, statutes are easier to navigate than cases, precisely because they are codifications of legal principles and are drafted with the intent to organize and simplify those principles. Many of the challenges associated with reading opinions—sorting out who the parties are, understanding the story, extracting the specific rules, understanding the court's reasoning—do not exist when reading

---

3. By now, your law professors have most likely explained the distinction between common-law rules and statutory rules.

statutes. Nonetheless, statutes are not always well-written, and it is helpful to have a strategy for reading them closely and actively.

One effective strategy for reading a statute closely and actively is to "diagram" it: to break it into its component parts. There are several parts you should always look for: (1) the subject, verb, and object (if any) of each sentence; (2) the operative words (may, must, shall, etc.); and (3) conjunctive and disjunctive terms (and, or, except, unless, etc.). As you diagram the statute, be sure to notate what you find in a visual format that will be useful when you need to return to the statute during your pre-writing process.

For example, S.C. Code Ann. 36-1-202(d) might be diagrammed as follows:

Figure 6-4   Diagram of First Sentence of S.C. Code Ann. § 36-1-202(d)

A *person* [who — subject]

"*notifies*" or "*gives*" [does what — verb]

a *notice or notification* [what — direct object]

to *another person* [to whom — indirect object]

by [how]

taking such steps as may be *reasonably required* to inform the other person *in ordinary course*[4]

whether or not the other person *actually comes to know* of it.

The highlighting isolates the phrases that, taken together, provide the rule about when and how notice is given in a business context. You might choose to use different color highlighters to visually separate the various components, or you might find another method that is efficient for you.⬤ The key is to *pay attention to every word* and visually identify the component parts in a useful way.

⬤ Because reading statutes is a task you will do often as a law student and as a lawyer, you might find it helpful to create your own template for diagramming statutes. Many legal research and legal writing texts offer suggestions for how to develop a useful template.

Exercise 6-6

"Diagram" subsection (e) of S.C. Code Ann. § 36-1-202, reprinted on page 84 above, using a helpful method of visually separating out the components. Then write a sentence or two describing your preliminary assessment of how this subsection relates to Ms. Ward's situation.

---

4. As with reading cases, reading statutes closely and actively may require you to stop periodically to look up legal terms of art to get a deeper understanding of their meaning. "In ordinary course" is one such term.

Your close, active reading of subsections (d) and (e) makes it clear that the South Carolina legislature has adopted as part of its commercial code the common-law rule about notice and receipt that was articulated in *Rosenthal*. Subsection (d) codifies the portion of the "mailbox rule" of *Rosenthal* that specifies how proper notice is given. Subsection (e) codifies the presumption of receipt of notice in *Rosenthal* and specifically lays out two ways that that receipt can occur: (1) the recipient has actual notice (the "comes to his attention" language); or (2) the notice is "duly delivered" at the business address given by the recipient. You should recognize immediately that it is the second of these methods of receipt that will be the focus of your later analysis of Ms. Ward's situation.

At this point in your close, active reading, you have before you a carefully notated U.S. Supreme Court case and a diagrammed portion of the South Carolina Commercial Code that applies to Ms. Ward's situation. As you have been reading, your mind should have begun to percolate with ideas about how Ms. Ward's situation might be resolved. You are not ready to answer her question yet; you still need to (1) finish your close, active reading; (2) identify the key categories of fact within the authorities that will determine the outcome (see Chapter 7); and (3) analyze Ms. Ward's facts in light of those categories (see Chapter 8). Nonetheless, you've made significant progress toward understanding the legal principles that will govern your analysis.

The final authority you need to read closely and actively is *White v. Holiday Kamper & Boats,* the relevant portions of which appear on pages 84–88. As usual, you should begin your reading by making careful notes on the story: who the parties are, what facts led to their dispute, etc. You should note that the lawsuit was filed by Bevis and Georgia White, the owners of an expensive but slightly used RV, against three defendants: the retailer who sold the RV, the manufacturer of the RV, and the bank that provided the financing. The RV had numerous ongoing problems, and the Whites repeatedly tried to contact Fleetwood, the RV's manufacturer, by telephone and by mail, to assert their rights to have the RV repaired under a warranty they had purchased from Fleetwood. However, they got no response from Fleetwood, and they eventually filed a breach of warranty claim.

Note that not all of the key facts of the Whites' story appear in the Factual and Procedural Background section. Not until section V.D. of the opinion, in which the court discusses the warranty claim, do you learn the key fact that Fleetwood claimed it never received any notification of the alleged breach of warranty. This is a good illustration of the principle that you often will not get the "full story" without closely and actively reading the entire opinion. Here, it isn't until you read the last portion of the *White* opinion that you can see how similar the Whites' story is to Ms. Ward's story with regard to the warranty aspect. In both cases, the facts involve a claim made under an active warranty and in both cases, the warrantor denied ever receiving notice of the claim.

In addition to the story itself, there are other aspects of this opinion that are important for you to understand as you closely and actively read. For example, the opinion contains a lengthy discussion of the applicable standard of review. It also contains a notation that the opinion is not reported. Further, the caption itself indicates that the case was decided by the United States District Court of South Carolina, a federal court, but in the opinion itself, the court applied the state law of South Carolina to decide the warranty claim. This should prompt you to investigate whether Ms. Ward's warranty claim also belongs in federal court.[5] While none of these aspects of the *White* opinion are critical to your factual analysis of Ms. Ward's case, they provide valuable context for your inquiry into how the *White* decision unfolds and how it impacts Ms. Ward's case. Thus, you cannot afford to skip over these aspects of this or any opinion during your close, active reading.

That said, of course the key portion of the opinion for your purposes is Part V.D. in which the court addresses the Whites' breach of warranty claim. In your close, active reading of that portion, you should recognize that the court does not actually determine whether the Whites' claim is valid; that decision is left for the factfinder to make at a later point in the proceedings. The key determinations here, and the ones that will be relevant to Ms. Ward's situation, are (1) that the Whites did all they were required to do under the South Carolina commercial code to give notice to Fleetwood that the RV was defective, and (2) that Fleetwood's denial of receipt of notice was ineffective.

More specifically, the court reasoned that the Whites' actions of telephoning Fleetwood three times and mailing the notice to Fleetwood at the address in the warranty book were sufficient to meet the statutory requirements of S.C. Code Ann. § 36-1-201 (now § 36-1-202(d)) for giving notice, thereby triggering the presumption of receipt by Fleetwood. At this point, you may find yourself thinking, "That sounds a lot like Ms. Ward's case." Good! Let this thought continue to percolate in your mind as you move forward.

Upon completion of your close, active reading of the three authorities — *Rosenthal,* the relevant South Carolina commercial code section, and *White* — you should have a good set of detailed notes upon which to base your remaining pre-writing work. Again, consider

---

5. This is a civil procedure question and is probably beyond the scope of what you've studied in these early weeks of law school. Thus, you will probably need to consult your civil procedure professor, or your legal writing professor, to learn more about the relationship between federal and state court jurisdiction.

how far you have come from the time you first received your commission in Ms. Ward's case. Initially, you probably sensed that she should have some recourse against Major Appliances, Inc. for its refusal to honor her warranty claim, but you had no legal basis for going forward to assist her. Now, based on your pre-writing work, you know that there is a statutory provision, backed up by case law, that supports an argument that she has done everything she needs to do to assert a valid warranty claim. You're doing exactly what a practicing lawyer would do to help Ms. Ward.

In fact, your work so far has been so productive that you may think the answer to Ms. Ward's question is already clear — Major Appliances, Inc. owes her a new washing machine or the money to buy one. But — and this is key — you must still fully analyze her issue to confirm this preliminary conclusion. That is, you must specifically compare the details of Ms. Ward's story to the details of the statutory requirements and the cases you've read.

In sum, arriving at a thorough understanding of the relevant authorities in any scenario will likely require multiple readings of each authority: one with no markings (or very limited markings); one with thorough notations of every significant point; and perhaps even additional readings as you seek to clarify the connections between the authorities. Before you continue your pre-writing process, you should review your detailed notations about the authorities ⭕ to satisfy yourself that your close, active reading has led to a deep understanding of (1) what each authority says, including the specific legal principles, or rules, that are contained in it; (2) how the authorities relate to each other; and (3) how they relate to and help you refine your narrow issue.⭕

If you have done a careful job at this stage, you should be eager to keep going; you know that you are getting closer to arriving at an answer to your client's question. Your next step will be to bring all of your current knowledge together, in an organized form, so that you can complete the final analysis of your narrow issue.

⭕ Your detailed notations may be written on the cases themselves or listed on a separate page. You should use whatever method permits you to access the important information without having to reread the authorities. And you certainly cannot rely on your memory when you need to review the details of many different authorities.

⭕ Did your notes on the Segway authorities and the washing machine authorities contain all of the information set forth above? If not, you may have concluded your close, active reading too soon. You should not feel discouraged about this; the more experience you gain as a legal reader, the more adept you will become at extracting key information. For example, a typical first-year student might completely miss the important point in *Shipley* that operating a child's scooter requires repetitive contact with the ground.

Chapter 6 Recap

What written product(s) do you now have to assist you as you go forward in your pre-writing process?

Segway scenario:
- Bulleted list of aspects of the story that seem important and the questions the story raises in your mind.
- Completed template summarizing parameters of specific assignment(s).
- Tentative research plan.
- Record of research results.
- *Detailed notes about each authority, either written on the printed version of the authority or compiled in a separate document.*

Washing machine scenario:
- Bulleted list of aspects of the story that seem important and the questions the story raises in your mind.
- Timeline of key events.
- Completed template summarizing parameters of specific assignment(s).
- Tentative research plan.
- Record of research results.
- *Detailed notes about each authority, either written on the printed version of the authority or compiled in a separate document.*

Where are you in terms of issue formulation?

Segway scenario:
- Broad question: Can the charge against Mr. Byrd stick (did he violate the red-light statute)?
- Preliminary narrow issue: Was the Segway he was riding "a vehicle such as an automobile"?
- Note: I didn't find any Segway cases; the cases address two other "vehicles" (toy scooter and moped) that I will need to compare to the Segway.
- *Narrower issue: Do the characteristics of a Segway, including its speed, weight, and potential for harm, make it "a vehicle such as an automobile" under the red-light statute? (Need to figure out how the Segway is like or unlike the toy scooter and the moped discussed in the cases.)*

Washing machine scenario:
- Broad question: Does Major Appliances, Inc. have to honor the extended warranty (give Ms. Ward new washer or $)?
- Preliminary narrow issue: How does the timing of events affect the outcome?

- Note: To answer the preliminary narrow issue, I will need to look at both common law and the U.C.C.
- *Narrower issue: Does Ms. Ward's timely mailing of her warranty claim to Major Appliances, Inc. preclude Major Appliances, Inc. from denying the claim by alleging that it was never received?*

Independent Practice Exercise 6-1

Having executed your research plan for Dr. McMahon's scenario, and having filled in the template suggested in Figure 5-1 (or your own template), you have probably located the following authorities you will need to read and assess:

- North Carolina General Statutes § 75-4.

- *New Hanover Rent-A-Car, Inc. v. Martinez*, 525 S.E.2d 487 (N.C. Ct. App. 2000).

- *Yaggy v. B.V.D. Co., Inc.*, 173 S.E.2d 496 (N.C. Ct. App. 1970).

Don't worry if your research record doesn't include all of these authorities; you will get better at locating the most relevant authorities for your problem and commission as you become a more experienced law student. For purposes of this Exercise, you should assume that the above authorities are the most relevant.

Print the above authorities and arrange them in a logical order. Then do an initial linear reading of each one, without making notes (other than what is necessary to remind you which parts of the authorities you need to read closely and actively).

Then, closely and actively read the authorities, making thorough notes. These notes might include paraphrases, lists, briefs, or written notations on the authorities themselves. You will return to these notes to complete Independent Practice Exercise 7-1 at the end of Chapter 7. Consider whether your close, active reading enables you to further refine your narrow issue; if so, write down the refined narrow issue.

Independent Practice Exercise 6-2

Having executed your research plan for Mr. Clark's scenario, and having filled in the template suggested in Figure 5-1 (or your own template), you have probably located the following authorities you will need to read and assess:

- Strong's North Carolina Index 4th, *Burglary & Unlawful Breakings* § 1.

- Strong's North Carolina Index 4th, *Burglary & Unlawful Breakings* § 3.
- North Carolina General Statutes § 14-51.
- North Carolina General Statutes § 14-52.
- *State v. Jones*, 655 S.E.2d 915 (N.C. Ct. App. 2008).
- *Martinez v. State*, 700 So. 2d 142 (Fla. Ct. App. 1997).
- *State v. Merritt*, 463 S.E.2d 590 (N.C. Ct. App. 1995).
- *State v. Fields*, 337 S.E.2d 518 (N.C. 1985).

Don't worry if your research record doesn't include all of these authorities; you will get better at locating the most relevant authorities for your problem and commission as you become a more experienced law student. For purposes of this Exercise, you should assume that the above authorities are the most relevant.

Print the above authorities and arrange them in a logical order. Then do an initial linear reading of each one, without making notes (other than what is necessary to remind you which parts of the authorities you need to read closely and actively).

Then, closely and actively read the authorities, making thorough notes. These notes might include paraphrases, lists, briefs, or written notations on the authorities themselves. You will return to these notes to complete Independent Practice Exercise 7-2 at the end of Chapter 7. Consider whether your close, active reading enables you to further refine your narrow issue; if so, write down the refined narrow issue.

Independent Practice Exercise 6-3

Having executed your research plan for Mr. Mordino's scenario, and having filled in the template suggested in Figure 5-1 (or your own template), you have probably located the following authorities you will need to read and assess:

- *Wong-Leong v. Hawaiian Independent Refinery, Inc.*, 879 P.2d 538 (Haw. 1994).
- *State v. Hoshijo*, 76 P.3d 550 (Haw. 2003).
- Restatement (Second) of Agency § 228.
- *Hughes v. Mayoral*, 721 F. Supp. 2d 947 (D. Haw. 2010).

Don't worry if your research record doesn't include all of these authorities; you will get better at locating the most relevant authorities for your problem and commission as you become a more experienced law student. For purposes of this Exercise, you should assume that the above authorities are the most relevant.

Print the above authorities and arrange them in a logical order. Then do an initial linear reading of each one, without making notes (other than what is necessary to remind you which parts of the authorities you need to read closely and actively).

Then, closely and actively read the authorities, making thorough notes. These notes might include paraphrases, lists, briefs, or written notations on the authorities themselves. You will return to these notes to complete Independent Practice Exercise 7-3 at the end of Chapter 7. Consider whether your close, active reading enables you to further refine your narrow issue; if so, write down the refined narrow issue.

Independent Practice Exercise 6-4

Having executed your research plan for Mr. Khan's scenario, and having filled in the template suggested in Figure 5-1 (or your own template), you have probably located the following authorities you will need to read and assess:

- The Visual Artists Rights Act (VARA), 17 U.S.C. §§ 101, 106A.
- *Cmty. for Creative Non-Violence v. Reid*, 490 U.S. 730 (1989).
- *Carter v. Helmsley-Spear, Inc.*, 71 F.3d 77 (2d Cir. 1995).
- *Forward v. Thorogood*, 985 F.2d 604 (1st Cir. 1993).
- *Martin v. City of Indianapolis*, 982 F. Supp. 625 (S.D. Ind. 1997).
- *Sterpetti v. E-Brands Acquisition, LLC*, No. 6:04-CV-1843-ORL-3DA, 2006 WL 1046949, 2006 U.S. Dist. LEXIS 21407 (M.D. Fla. Apr. 20, 2006).

Don't worry if your research record doesn't include all of these authorities; you will get better at locating the most relevant authorities for your problem and commission as you become a more experienced law student. For purposes of this Exercise, you should assume that the above authorities are the most relevant.

Print the above authorities and arrange them in a logical order. Then do an initial linear reading of each one, without making notes (other than what is necessary to remind you which parts of the authorities you need to read closely and actively).

Then, closely and actively read the authorities, making thorough notes. These notes might include paraphrases, lists, briefs, or written notations on the authorities themselves. You will return to these notes to complete Independent Practice Exercise 7-4 at the end of Chapter 7. Consider whether your close, active reading enables you to further refine your narrow issue; if so, write down the refined narrow issue.

Chapter 7

Building a Bridge Between Reading and Analysis

If you have done a careful job of reading the authorities closely and actively, your mind should be full of ideas about how the authorities relate to each other and how they may direct you toward the answer to your narrow issue. However, you are not yet ready to *decide* the answer to your narrow issue. There is a critical step of the pre-writing process that serves as a bridge between your close, active reading and your eventual analysis of the narrow issue: identifying the *categories of fact* that will govern your eventual analysis.

In some legal scenarios, it is possible to resolve your narrow issue by simply applying the language of the rule to your client's facts—that is, by using *rule-based reasoning*. However, in many scenarios, rule-based reasoning does not suffice, because there are aspects of your client's scenario that do not fit neatly into the rule. In these situations, you must use *analogical reasoning* to resolve your narrow issue.

Put simply, *analogical reasoning* involves comparing similar, but not identical, sets of facts. Lawyers often must resort to analogical reasoning because the narrow issues they must analyze involve scenarios that are similar, but not identical, to the precedential authorities that govern the issues.

In a practical sense, you will need to use analogical reasoning in many of your early legal writing assignments (and every time a professor poses a hypothetical in a casebook class). Your goal is to compare and contrast facts in the relevant categories, so that you can logically determine whether the result in your legal writing scenario, or your hypothetical, will be the same as or different from the results in the precedential cases.

Thus, from a pre-writing perspective, it is essential that you correctly identify the relevant categories of fact in the authorities you've read *before* you proceed to analyze your own particular set of facts. In the remainder of this chapter, you will learn how to identify the relevant categories of fact within a group of authorities and how to create a useful visual representation of the results of your work.

7.1 Identifying Analogical Categories

Sorting facts into categories comes naturally to most adults. Imagine that the following fruits are set before you: a red apple, a green apple, a lime, and a lemon. If the relevant category is type of fruit, you can easily determine that the red apple and the green apple belong in one subcategory (non-citrus) and the lime and the lemon in another subcategory (citrus). If the relevant category is color, you can just as easily determine that the green apple and the lime belong in one subcategory (green), the red apple in a second subcategory (red), and the lemon in a third subcategory (yellow).

While sorting facts into categories may come naturally, it is not always as easy as the above hypothetical suggests. For example, suppose you are handed a list of names—Catherine, Carl, Camille, Curt, Caroline, and Chris—and asked to sort the names according to gender. At first glance, you might place Catherine, Camille, and Caroline into one subcategory (female) and Carl and Curt into another subcategory (male).

But what about Chris? By itself, the name Chris doesn't fit neatly into either subcategory; you would need more information to properly categorize it. If you were told that Chris is short for Christopher, you could then place Chris in the male subcategory. If you were told instead that Chris is short for Christina, you could then place Chris in the female subcategory.

And what if you were told that Carl refers to a person who was born Carla but now self-identifies as male and is in the process of medically transitioning from female to male? Would you keep Carl in the male subcategory, or would you move Carl to the female subcategory?

Translating this concept into a more "legal" setting, suppose you serve as outside counsel for a homeless shelter that has a policy requiring that male clients must sleep in separate quarters from female clients. And suppose Carl has come to the shelter seeking temporary housing in the male sleeping quarters. On the shelter's intake form, Carl left the "gender" section blank, and when the shelter's director asked him about this, Carl willingly shared that he was born female but self-identifies as a male and is in the process of medically transitioning. The director has called you to ask whether she must grant Carl's request to be housed in the shelter's male sleeping quarters.

In this example, the legal "rule" — the shelter's current policy — clearly lays out two subcategories (male and female) within the larger category of gender. But placing Carl into one of those two subcategories is a complex task. It's complex because of the specific facts you know about Carl's gender identification, and it's complex because how you categorize Carl has implications for many constituencies: for Carl personally, for other binary and non-binary transgender individuals seeking shelter, for cisgender individuals staying at the shelter, for the shelter's staff, for private donors who support the shelter, and for legislators who appropriate funds for the shelter.⓫

> ⓫ Often, legal rules evolve precisely because the categories of fact they are based on are insufficient to encompass new or unforeseen facts. In this hypothetical, you might determine that instead of forcing Carl into one of the two subcategories on which the shelter's current policy is based, the better approach would be to change the policy to allow for a new subcategory into which Carl fits comfortably.

As a legal analyst, you will regularly encounter situations in which it is not crystal clear how to sort certain facts into the categories created by the governing legal rules. Even more problematic, you will sometimes encounter situations in which the governing legal rules do not clearly express what the relevant categories of fact are. In these situations, before you can even begin to categorize the facts, you must identify what those relevant categories are. This can be one of the most difficult tasks a new law student faces.

At its core, properly identifying the relevant categories requires you to (1) carefully review the notes you took during your close, active reading of the authorities; (2) consider the similarities and differences among the authorities, in terms of their facts, their reasoning, and their results; and (3) identify the kinds of facts (and perhaps policies) that seemed to drive the decisions in the authorities. By identifying *what really mattered* to the courts in the precedential cases, you can begin to construct the relevant categories into which you will eventually sort the facts of your own scenario.

Suppose you encounter the following holding in an opinion: "We have reviewed the banana, the lemon, the orange, and the tennis ball, and we hold that the banana must be excluded from this group." Suppose that the opinion contains no clear rule statement identifying the relevant category (the category that drove its decision to exclude the banana). In order to properly identify the relevant category, you must determine *what really mattered* to the court. You can eliminate some potential categories by looking at the result. For example, the relevant category cannot be food, because the court included two foods—the lemon and the orange—but excluded the banana. The relevant category cannot be color, because the court included two yellow objects—the lemon and the tennis ball—but excluded the yellow banana.

So what is left? The relevant category *must be* shape; the court included three round (or nearly round) objects—the lemon, the orange, and the tennis ball—but excluded the non-round (C-shaped) object—the banana. Knowing that shape is the relevant category is essential to your later analysis of your own facts. If your question involves a red marble, for example, you will be able to safely conclude, using analogical reasoning, that the marble will be included; since shape is what matters, and the marble is round, its other characteristics (color, non-food) are unimportant.

The Segway scenario provides a good example of how to proceed when the relevant categories are not explicitly stated in the authorities. Recall that neither the *Shipley* case nor the *Monroe* case articulates a clear rule outlining what categories are relevant in deciding whether a particular vehicle is "a vehicle such as an automobile." However, from the holdings in the cases, we know that a child's scooter is not "a vehicle such an automobile," but a moped is. Thus, to identify the relevant categories, we must examine the court's reasoning in each case—both the explicit reasoning and the implicit reasoning—to see what facts *really mattered*.

If you took good notes on the cases during your close, active reading, you should already have a preliminary idea of what categories of fact were important to the court's decisions about whether the vehicles in question were covered by the red-light statute. In *Shipley*, for example, the court discussed the speed and weight of the child's toy scooter and ultimately held that the scooter was "too light and too slow" to cause harm to other motorists and thus was not "a vehicle such as an automobile" for purposes of the red-light statute. Based on *Shipley*'s reasoning, your current relevant categories would likely be *speed*, *weight*, and *potential harm to others*.

However, in the Segway scenario, unlike the banana example, you have a second mandatory authority—the *Monroe* case—that will shape your list of relevant categories. Like the *Shipley* court, the *Monroe* court considered *speed*, *weight*, and *potential harm to others* in its reasoning, but it expanded the *potential harm* category to include harm to the operator as well as other motorists. More importantly, the *Monroe* court added another crucial category. Recall that the *Monroe* court included the following statement in its reasoning:

While the presence of the motor alone is not dispositive, surely the legislature intended that a vehicle that could be ridden without any

> contact with the ground and that was usually self-propelled presented enough danger to crossing traffic and to the driver himself to be subject to the vehicular traffic laws.

This statement makes it clear that an important category — perhaps the deciding category — is *how the vehicle is normally operated*. Thus, at this point, your list of relevant categories is as follows: *speed, weight, potential harm to operator and others*, and *how the vehicle is normally operated*.

As you review your notes on the cases, you will likely discover that some of the aspects you initially thought were important did not *really matter* to the court's determinations about whether the vehicle in question was or was not "a vehicle such as an automobile." These aspects of the cases should not clutter your list of relevant categories. For example, you may have noted that in both cases, no one was hurt by the driver's actions. Or you may have noted that the moped driver in *Monroe* was apparently impaired, while the *Shipley* driver was not. However, at this point you should recognize that neither of these aspects of the cases *really mattered* to the outcome of the cases. Thus, *impairment of driver* and *actual harm to driver or others* would not make your list of relevant categories.

You may be uncertain about whether some aspects of the cases belong on your list of relevant categories. At this point, if you cannot definitively exclude a particular category from your list, you should include it, even though you are not sure exactly how it will play into your later analysis. For example, in both *Shipley* and *Monroe*, the court explicitly stated that the presence or absence of a motor was not *dispositive*; but in both cases the court nonetheless *factored that into* its decision. Moreover, whether a vehicle is motorized is related to *how the vehicle is normally operated*, which you've already identified as perhaps the most crucial category. So it is perfectly fine to include *whether the vehicle is motorized* on your list of relevant categories.

The importance of this step in the pre-writing process — identifying the relevant categories — cannot be overstated. Only by correctly identifying *all of the relevant categories* from the authorities can you be sure that when you turn to the facts of your own case, you will be focusing on every aspect of it that matters.⬤ In the Segway example, if your list of relevant categories included only the most obvious ones — *speed* and *weight* — your prediction about the Segway would be easy; its speed and weight make it much more analogous to the moped than to the child's scooter, so it should be covered by the red-light statute. But this analysis, while logical, would be incomplete (and therefore

⬤ Identifying the relevant categories is difficult; it requires deep thought and creativity. Each new legal problem requires you to undertake this categorizing with a fresh mind; it should not be a rote exercise.

unreliable), because it ignores the crucial category articulated in *Monroe: how the vehicle is normally operated.*

The task of identifying the relevant categories of fact that will drive your analysis is sometimes more straightforward than in the Segway scenario. Sometimes the language in the authorities explicitly articulates the relevant categories. Such is the case in the washing machine scenario. Recall that the *Rosenthal* opinion stated the common law rule that proper mailing of a document gives rise to a presumption that the document was received in the ordinary course of business. This common law rule was eventually codified in the South Carolina commercial code, S.C. Code Ann. § 36-1-202, the purpose of which is to "regularize" business transactions within the state. Thus, the Code replaced the common law rule in *Rosenthal.* Later, the *White* court applied the then-existing version of § 36-1-202 to a particular set of facts that was similar to Ms. Ward's facts.

Reading these authorities together, you learned that a presumption of receipt of notice arises when the person seeking to give notice does the following:

- addresses the notice properly;
- affixes proper postage; and
- takes actions that accomplish mailing in the "ordinary course of business."

These actions are the relevant categories of fact that will govern your analysis of Ms. Ward's claim.

7.2 Creating a Visual Representation of Your Analogical Categories

Once you have identified the relevant categories of fact that will govern the analysis of your issue, the next step in your pre-writing process is to construct a visual representation of how the facts of the authorities fit into those categories. Although you have already made notes about each separate authority, and you have *thought about* their facts in relation to the categories, you shouldn't try to keep all of that information in your head. And even if you could do so, it wouldn't allow you to see the relationships between the authorities in a way that will deepen your later analysis.

One very common way to create a visual representation of how the information in the authorities relates to the relevant categories is to construct a basic table with rows and columns. In the far left-hand column you would list the authorities that have something to say about the categories you decided were relevant (so that you end up with a row for each authority); each remaining column will be devoted to one of the categories you identified.

In the Segway scenario, you have identified the following relevant categories: *speed, weight, potential harm to driver and others*, and *how the vehicle is normally operated*. Thus, the skeleton of your table might look like the one in Figure 7-1 below:

Figure 7-1   Skeleton Table for Segway Analysis

	type of vehicle	speed	weight	potential harm to operator and others	how normally operated	"vehicle such as auto"? yes or no
16 Gra. Gen. Stat. § 2345 (2016).						
Shipley, 872 S.E.2d 278 (Gra. Ct. App. 2017).						
Monroe, 872 S.E.2d 425 (Gra. Ct. App. 2017).						
Byrd (my case)						

Note the following important features of Figure 7-1:

- It includes a separate column labeled "type of vehicle" to make that basic information more visible.

- It includes a row for the red-light statute, because that statute provides the standard — "a vehicle such as an automobile" — against which all other vehicles must be measured.

- It includes a row labeled "Byrd (my case)" because the ultimate goal of your analysis is to be able to answer yes or no as to whether a Segway is "a vehicle such as an automobile." Although you may already be able to fill in certain cells on this row, you won't be able to complete this row until you've gone through the steps in the analysis stage of your pre-writing process, which are covered in Chapter 8.

- It includes a separate column labeled "vehicle such as an auto? yes or no" simply because you need some place to record the result in each case.

Once you have constructed the skeleton of your table, you are ready to begin the important work of filling in the cells. This is not a rote, fill-in-the-blank exercise, but a creative process where you start with the obvious but then dig deeper. For example, a beginning law student might initially fill in the table as shown in Figure 7-2:

Figure 7-2   Initial Effort at Creating a Visual for Segway Categorization

	type of vehicle	speed	weight	potential harm to operator and others	how normally operated	"vehicle such as auto"? yes or no
16 Gra. Gen. Stat. § 2345 (2016).	auto-mobile	fast	very heavy	great potential for danger	motor	yes
Shipley, 872 S.E.2d 278 (Gra. Ct. App. 2017).	scooter	slow	very light	"no danger" to other vehicles	no motor	no
Monroe, 872 S.E.2d 425 (Gra. Ct. App. 2017).	moped	fast	heavy	"enough danger" to other vehicles and driver	motor	yes
Byrd (my case)	Segway					

Note the following aspects of Figure 7-2:

- We were able to fill in the "automobile" row based on our own knowledge, not on anything in the authorities themselves.

- We didn't cut and paste chunks of the cases themselves; we used our own words and retained only the key language from the cases, which we indicated with quotation marks.

- We darkened the cells that need to be developed further. The information in those cells is correct and reflects what most beginning legal analysts would include.

However, a more thorough thought process would likely result in a table that looks more like Figure 7-3:

Figure 7-3 Visual for Segway Categorization Reflecting Deeper Thinking

	type of vehicle	speed	weight	potential harm to operator and others	how normally operated	"vehicle such as auto"? yes or no
16 Gra. Gen. Stat. § 2345 (2016).	automobile	fast	very heavy	great potential for danger	motor & operator pressing gas pedal (self-propelled)	yes
Shipley, 872 S.E.2d 278 (Gra. Ct. App. 2017).	child's toy scooter	much slower than auto	much lighter than auto – can be lifted by child	"no danger" to other vehicles	no motor; can move "only if pushed" repetitively by one leg of operator (not self-propelled)	no
Monroe, 872 S.E.2d 425 (Gra. Ct. App. 2017).	moped	slower than auto but faster than child's scooter (15 mph max)	lighter than auto (approx. 100 lbs) but heavier than child's scooter	"enough danger" to other vehicles and driver	motor; operator must turn throttle; requires no contact betw. operator & ground; usually "self-propelled"	yes
Byrd (my case)	Segway					

Looking at the information in the shaded columns, you can see that Figure 7-3 reflects a much deeper thought process that requires creative energy. Filling in the cells of a table is not a linear process. What you put in one cell may change your thinking about the content of a cell you filled in earlier; you will find yourself frequently modifying the various cells throughout the process of completing the table. For example, you might not have thought to include the "(not self-propelled)" information for *Shipley* until you included the "usually self-propelled" information for *Monroe*.

While some of the highlighted information is explicitly stated in the cases, much of it is implied, and thus you will have to use other techniques to capture that information. For example, Figure 7-2 labels the *Shipley* vehicle "scooter" because that is the term the court used. But that simple term does not describe the vehicle in enough depth to allow for a meaningful comparison to other vehicles, including a Segway. Although the *Shipley* court does describe the scooter as a "child's toy" that belonged to the defendant's young son, it does not *explicitly* connect that description to the weight and speed of the scooter or to its mode of operation. You must think more deeply to draw that connection yourself.

An even stronger example of the importance of thinking deeply is illustrated in the column labeled "how normally operated." In Figure 7-2, the information in that column is limited to the presence or absence of a motor. However, both courts make it clear that the presence or absence of a motor is not dispositive; so if your "how normally operated" column only includes whether or not the vehicle is motorized, your table isn't complete enough to permit a thorough analysis of a Segway.

Arriving at the important information in the "how normally operated" column requires more than just reviewing your notes on the cases. It requires you to use some creativity; perhaps you will need to "stare out the window" for a while to allow yourself to visualize how the various vehicles are operated. If you are artistically inclined, you might draw a sketch of the various vehicles and their operators. If you are an oral learner, you might say to yourself, "So how does this vehicle really operate?" and then answer yourself. Whatever your technique, you need to recognize that the key information in this column involves not just the vehicle itself (is it motorized?) but also the interaction between the operator and the vehicle as a unit.

Most beginning law students would likely be satisfied with a table like the one in figure 7-2, and it is not impossible to analyze the Segway scenario using just Figure 7-2. But such an analysis would be shallow, and the resulting prediction could be vulnerable if it is challenged by the creator of the table in Figure 7-3, who has dug more deeply into the meaning of the authorities. Thus, when creating a table as part of your pre-writing process, it is fine to begin by looking for what is explicit in the authorities, but you must then dig deeper. It is rare indeed to encounter a situation in which all of the relevant, precise information is explicit in the authorities. A good legal analyst understands the need to "read between the lines" to extract the deeper implications of the courts' reasoning.

However, you should not be discouraged if you reacted to the table in Figure 7-3 by thinking, "I would never have thought of all of that myself!" The difference between the tables in Figure 7-2 and Figure 7-3 represents a major leap forward, from being a complete novice law student to an advanced beginner. To achieve advanced beginner status, you will need to practice the pre-writing techniques described in the first six chapters of this book many times and in many different kinds of scenarios.

How much time and effort you should spend on the pre-writing step of creating a visual depends on how many narrow issues you need to analyze to be able to answer your client's broad question and how complex those narrow issues are. The Segway example, though it is complex in its details, addresses only one narrow issue, and the relevant details can be visually summarized in one table. This will not always be the case. For example, your question might involve the interpretation of a statute with three elements. If so, you might decide that you can access the relevant information more easily later by separating it into three tables. If one of your cases addresses all three elements, you might include a row for that case on each table.

Creating a table is but one alternative for visually summarizing the key information from the authorities. The "best" method of visually representing the authorities may vary, depending on how the authorities relate to each other.

For example, in the washing machine scenario, all three authorities—*Rosenthal*, the South Carolina code section, and *White*—say the same thing: that when the person seeking to give notice under a warranty takes certain actions, a presumption of receipt by the addressee arises. Thus, your visual would be adequate if it simply listed the required actions and left room for you to fill in Ms. Ward's facts in the analysis stage.

However, it might be wise to add a column reminding you that in the *White* case, the court found that all of the statutory requirements were met in a fact pattern that was nearly identical to Ms. Ward's facts. While analyzing Ms. Ward's case does not require you to compare and contrast her facts with the facts in *White*, you might still include *White* in your visual, because it reinforces your application of the statutory requirements to Ms. Ward's facts. Thus, your visual for the washing machine scenario might look something like Figure 7-4 below:

Figure 7-4   Visual for Categorization in Washing Machine Scenario

Requirements of S.C. Code	*White* case	Ms. Ward's case
Document properly addressed	✓	
Proper postage affixed to document	✓	
Document deposited in mail "in ordinary course" of business	✓	

In sum, if you have done a careful, thorough job of creating your visual representation, in whatever form it takes, you will have sharpened your thinking in at least three important ways. First, you will have a deeper understanding of each authority. Second, you will have identified the categories that will likely present the greatest challenges as you seek to answer your own question. And third, you will have a clearer understanding of the relevant similarities and differences among the authorities in those categories, paving the way for a later comparison between those authorities and your situation. At the conclusion of this stage in your pre-writing process, you will have created a strong bridge to move you from your close, active reading to your next step—analyzing your narrow issues.

Chapter 7 Recap

What written product(s) do you now have to assist you as you go forward in your pre-writing process?

Segway scenario:
- Bulleted list of aspects of the story that seem important and the questions the story raises in your mind.
- Completed template summarizing parameters of specific assignment(s).
- Tentative research plan.
- Record of research results.
- Detailed notes about each authority, either written on the printed version of the authority or compiled in a separate document.
- *Visual representation of analogical categories for use in later analysis.*

Washing machine scenario:
- Bulleted list of aspects of the story that seem important and the questions the story raises in your mind.
- Timeline of key events.
- Completed template summarizing parameters of specific assignment(s).
- Tentative research plan.
- Record of research results.
- Detailed notes about each authority, either written on the printed version of the authority or compiled in a separate document.
- *Visual representation of categories for use in later analysis.*

Where are you in terms of issue formulation?

Segway scenario:
- Broad question: Can the charge against Mr. Byrd stick (did he violate the red-light statute)?
- Preliminary narrow issue: Was the Segway he was riding "a vehicle such as an automobile"?
- Note: I didn't find any Segway cases; the cases address two other "vehicles" (toy scooter and moped) that I will need to compare to the Segway.
- Narrower issue: Do the characteristics of a Segway, including its speed, weight, and potential for harm, make it "a vehicle such as an automobile" under the red-light statute? (Need to figure out how the Segway is like or unlike the toy scooter and the moped discussed in the cases.)
- *Even narrower issue: Do the characteristics of a Segway make it "a vehicle such as an automobile" under the red-light statute in light of the relevant categories: speed, weight, potential harm, normal method of operation (motor? "usually self-propelled"? contact between operator and ground? bodily effort from operator?)?*

Washing machine scenario:
- Broad question: Does Major Appliances, Inc. have to honor the extended warranty (give Ms. Ward washer or $)?
- Preliminary narrow issue: How does the timing of events affect the outcome?
- Note: To answer the preliminary narrow issue, I will need to look at both common law and the U.C.C.
- Narrower issue: Does Ms. Ward's timely mailing of her warranty claim to Major Appliances, Inc. preclude Major Appliances, Inc. from denying the claim by alleging that it was never received?
- *Even narrower issue: Did Ms. Ward complete the necessary steps to raise the presumption of receipt of notice of warranty claim by Major Appliances, Inc. (properly address envelope, affix proper postage, deposit in mail in "ordinary course of business")?*

Independent Practice Exercise 7-1

In Chapter 7, you learned various techniques to help you build a bridge from your close, active reading of the important authorities for your problem to the analysis that will provide the best answer to the legal issues you are working on.

Review the notes you took during your close, active reading of the authorities identified on page 100 as important to the answer to Dr. McMahon's question. Then create a visual representation of (1) the relevant categories of fact that the authorities emphasize, and (2) the factual similarities and differences among the authorities and Dr. McMahon's scenario as they relate to those categories.

Independent Practice Exercise 7-2

In Chapter 7, you learned various techniques to help you build a bridge from your close, active reading of the important authorities for your problem to the analysis that will provide the best answer to the legal issues you are working on.

Review the notes you took during your close, active reading of the authorities identified on pages 100–101 as important to the answer to Mr. Clark's question. Then create a visual representation of (1) the relevant categories of fact that the authorities emphasize, and (2) the factual similarities and differences among the authorities and Mr. Clark's scenario as they relate to those categories.

Independent Practice Exercise 7-3

In Chapter 7, you learned various techniques to help you build a bridge from your close, active reading of the important authorities for your problem to the analysis that will provide the best answer to the legal issues you are working on.

Review the notes you took during your close, active reading of the authorities identified on page 101 as important to the answer to Mr. Mordino's question. Then create a visual representation of (1) the relevant categories of fact that the authorities emphasize, and (2) the factual similarities and differences among the authorities and Mr. Mordino's scenario as they relate to those categories.

Independent Practice Exercise 7-4

In Chapter 7, you learned various techniques to help you build a bridge from your close, active reading of the important authorities for your problem to the analysis that will provide the best answer to the legal issues you are working on.

Review the notes you took during your close, active reading of the authorities identified on page 102 as important to the answer to Mr. Khan's question. Then create a visual representation of (1) the relevant categories of fact that the authorities emphasize, and (2) the factual similarities and differences among the authorities and Mr. Khan's scenario as they relate to those categories.

Chapter 8

Analyzing Your Narrow Issues

8.1   Analysis Using Rule-Based Reasoning
8.2   Analysis Using Analogical Reasoning
8.3   Counteranalysis

The final step in your pre-writing process is to analyze your narrow issues. The term "analysis" is used very broadly and loosely in legal education, but in terms of the pre-writing process, it has a very specific meaning. Analysis is the culmination of the pre-writing process, where you decide how the narrow issues you've now identified would most likely be resolved, using all the relevant information you've gathered during the pre-writing process. Once you answer the narrow issues, you will be able to answer the broad question you were initially asked (Can the charge against Mr. Byrd "stick"? Can Ms. Ward get a new washing machine?).

The instinct of many beginning law students is to skip straight to this step—to posit an answer to the broad question very quickly. We hope the previous chapters have shown the folly of doing so. These quick answers are often based on intuition or opinion, neither of which is an adequate basis for legal analysis. When your supervising attorney asks you for the answer to a question, she does not want merely your intuition or your opinion; she wants an answer that is supported by thorough research; close, active reading; careful thinking as to the categories that matter and what the authorities have to say about them; and complete examination of how those categories intersect with the facts of your client's situation.

For example, your early intuition in Ms. Ward's situation may have been that Major Appliances, Inc. treated her unfairly: "Of course she should get a new washing machine." But imagine what would have happened if you had immediately called Major Appliances, Inc. and

119

said, "You're treating my client unfairly. She deserves a new machine." The likely response would have been, "We're sorry, but there's nothing we can do." But now that you understand the legal principles that govern Ms. Ward's situation, you are prepared to move forward with a professional legal analysis that you can use to convince Major Appliances, Inc. that a simple "We're sorry" is not going to suffice.

Another instinct of many beginning law students is to immediately think in terms of advocating a position that favors the client. This is a dangerous approach to legal analysis for at least two reasons. First, it may cause you to manipulate the facts to suit a desired outcome. Second, it may cause you to overlook certain "unfavorable" facts. While your ultimate commission may require you to advocate a particular position, you cannot do so fully or ethically without having first analyzed the question objectively to identify all possible outcomes and accurately predict the likely one. ○

The two examples used throughout this book illustrate the two different types of legal reasoning that lawyers use, either separately or in combination, to analyze legal issues: *rule-based reasoning* and *analogical reasoning*.

○ A good metaphor for legal analysis is learning math. Your math teacher would likely not be satisfied with just the "right answer." She would ask you to "show your work"— that is, to show each step you took to get from the problem to the ultimate answer. Like your math teacher, your supervising attorney expects you to "show your work." Without showing the steps you took to get to your conclusion, your analysis is useless to your reader.

8.1 Analysis Using Rule-Based Reasoning

The washing machine scenario presents an issue that can be analyzed using rule-based reasoning alone. Rule-based reasoning is sufficient when a direct application of the language of a rule to the facts of your client's situation suggests a clear result. Recall that your pre-writing work in Chapter 7 resulted in a simple visual representing the three steps required for giving notice of breach of warranty. That visual is reprinted below in Figure 8-1:

Figure 8-1   Visual for Categorization in Washing Machine Scenario

Requirements of S.C. Code	*White* case	Ms. Ward's case
Document properly addressed	✓	
Proper postage affixed to document	✓	
Document deposited in mail "in ordinary course" of business	✓	

Analyzing Ms. Ward's situation is a simple matter of applying the language from your visual to Ms. Ward's facts: she properly addressed the envelope containing the notice to Major Appliances, Inc.; she affixed proper postage to the envelope; and she deposited the envelope in the U.S. mail in the ordinary course of business by giving it to the clerk at the post office annex at Ace Hardware. Thus, using only rule-based reasoning, you can safely conclude that Ms. Ward's actions constituted "giving notice" under the South Carolina commercial code, triggering the presumption of receipt on the part of Major Appliances, Inc.

Even though analogizing to the facts of *Rosenthal* and *White* is not necessary to answer Ms. Ward's question, the time you spent reading and thinking about those cases was not wasted. *Rosenthal* helped you understand the common-law basis for codifying the presumption of receipt, and *White* confirmed that your plain-language reading of the statute is correct and supports your rule-based reasoning about how it applies in Ms. Ward's case.

Do not forget to record the results of your analysis. In Ms. Ward's case, this can be accomplished by checking off the items on your visual categorization, as shown in Figure 8-2 below:

Figure 8-2   Completed Visual for Categorization in Washing Machine Scenario

Requirements of S.C. Code	*White* case	Ms. Ward's case
Document properly addressed	✓	✓
Proper postage affixed to document	✓	✓
Document deposited in mail "in ordinary course" of business	✓	✓

8.2 Analysis Using Analogical Reasoning

Throughout your career in the law, and especially in your early legal education, *analogical reasoning* will be a vital tool in your analytical work. As noted in Chapter 7, the facts of your client's situation will rarely, if ever, be *identical* to the facts of the precedential authorities; so analogical reasoning will often be the only available method to answer your client's question. Fortunately, analogical reasoning is a rich process that will engage your intellect in a new and exciting way. Although new law students often complain that legal *writing* stifles creativity, the analysis step of the *pre-writing* process is highly creative when analogical reasoning is involved.

The Segway scenario used throughout this book is an excellent example of a scenario that cannot be fully analyzed without using analogical reasoning. You should *begin* your analysis of Mr. Byrd's case by using rule-based reasoning to determine that several elements of the red-light statute are clearly satisfied. Applying the language of the statute to Mr. Byrd's facts, you can easily determine that (1) Mr. Byrd fits within the broad category of "anyone"; (2) that he was "operating a vehicle" when he was riding the Segway; (3) that he was riding the Segway "on a public street"; and (4) that he did not stop at an intersection where "a steady read beam of light" signaled that forward travel was not allowed.

But the statutory element that gives rise to the narrow issue you've identified—whether the Segway is "a vehicle such as an automobile"— cannot be answered using rule-based reasoning. Neither the red-light statute itself nor *Shipley* or *Monroe* provides a clear answer to that question. Although there are some similarities between a Segway, an automobile, a child's scooter, and a moped, a Segway is not identical to any of those vehicles. Thus, you must use analogical reasoning to predict whether the judge trying Mr. Byrd's case will find that a Segway is "a vehicle such as an automobile."

As with the washing machine scenario, you likely had an initial reaction to Mr. Byrd's story as soon as you heard it. You might have thought, "Come on, it's a Segway; of course the statute doesn't apply to Mr. Byrd." Or, you might have thought, "Wow, that's dangerous. It makes sense for it to be illegal to run a red light on a Segway." There is nothing wrong with such reactions; in fact, they are entirely natural responses.

However, the entire pre-writing process is designed to force you to "test" your early reaction, not only to find out if it is correct, but also to understand why or why not, in a legal sense. Your supervising attorney expects a memo that answers the narrow issue and explains the thorough, precise analysis you went through to arrive at that answer. In the Segway scenario, a thorough, precise analysis requires analogizing the Segway to the vehicles in the precedential cases, focusing on the relevant categories of fact.

Your pre-writing work up to this point has paved the way for effective analogical reasoning. You have identified the relevant categories of fact in the precedential cases, and you have thought carefully about how the courts in those cases evaluated the facts in light of those categories. You even have a helpful visual capturing your thoughts. To complete your analysis, you must now return to Mr. Byrd's story.

One practical approach to analogical reasoning in Mr. Byrd's case is to return to the table you constructed and partially completed in Chapter 7 and fill in the cells with information about how Mr. Byrd's facts fit into the relevant categories. Completing your visual representation in this way will allow you to effectively compare and contrast Mr. Byrd's facts with the facts of *Shipley* and *Monroe*. This in turn will enable you to decide whether the Segway is more analogous to a moped or to a child's scooter. If the Segway is more analogous to the scooter, Mr. Byrd will not have to pay his ticket. If the Segway is more analogous to the moped, he will have to pay up.

Remember that you ultimately must convince your supervising attorney (and perhaps a judge, if the case gets that far) that your analogical reasoning is accurate, logical, and complete. You cannot simply make assumptions about your facts if you want your analysis to be precise and reliable.

For example, without a complete understanding of what a Segway i2 SE looks like and what makes it go, you can only guess at how to complete the "how normally operated" cell in your table. To guess at this would be especially dangerous, because as you've already discerned, how the vehicle normally operates is perhaps the most important category.⬤

Thus, to conduct an accurate, logical, and complete analysis, you may need to put your work on hold while you educate yourself about the exact specifications of the Segway i2 SE and about exactly how it operates. You cannot rely on your mental image of a Segway, on a TV commercial for Segway that you saw a month ago, or even on your initial research on the Segway website. Possible ways to educate yourself further as to the Segway i2 SE's exact operation would be to access the operator's manual online and to watch the manufacturer's instructional videos.

Assume that you access the Segway.com website and find the following information about the normal operation of the Segway i2 SE: First, it has two battery-powered electric motors. Second, it has a platform located between its two wheels, and the user stands on the platform. Third, it senses the lean of the rider and balances the rider by applying forces to the ground in the direction of the lean. When the rider leans forward, the Segway's motors push it forward; when the rider leans backward, the Segway goes in reverse; and when the rider stands up straight, the Segway stops moving.

Now that you have a fuller understanding of the relevant facts from your story, you're finally ready to dive in to the creative exercise of analogical reasoning! Go back to your table, and with your fuller understanding of the Segway i2 SE, start filling in the Segway row with the relevant information for each category. Figure 8-3 on the next page is one example of how you might do this.

In the Segway row, notice the question marks in the far-right column labeled "vehicle such as auto? yes or no." That cell represents the predicted answer to your question, which you cannot determine until you have completed the analysis. The second and third cells in the Segway row, speed and weight, can be completed easily if you have done your homework on the Segway i2 SE; in terms of both speed and weight, the Segway is nearly identical to the moped in *Monroe*.

The cell in the "potential harm to operator and others" column can also be completed fairly easily by returning to the reasoning in *Shipley* and *Monroe*. The *Shipley* court reasoned that the child's scooter was "too light and too slow" to present a danger to crossing vehicles,

⬤ You should not proceed with your analysis until you have the most complete understanding of the facts possible. There may be situations in which some of the factual information you need is simply not available. If so, you may have to rely on assumed facts to complete your comparison. However, in your written analysis, ethical considerations require you to explicitly disclose any factual assumptions you made while arriving at your prediction.

Figure 8-3   Partially Completed Table for Segway Analysis

	type of vehicle	speed	weight	potential harm to operator and others	how normally operated	"vehicle such as auto"? yes or no
16 Gra. Gen. Stat. § 2345 (2016).	auto-mobile	fast	very heavy	great potential for danger	motor & operator pressing gas pedal (self-propelled)	yes
Shipley, 872 S.E.2d 278 (Gra. Ct. App. 2017).	child's toy scooter	much slower than auto	much lighter than auto – can be lifted by child	"no danger" to other vehicles	no motor; can move "only if pushed" repetitively by one leg of operator (not self-propelled)	no
Monroe, 872 S.E.2d 425 (Gra. Ct. App. 2017).	moped	slower than auto but faster than child's scooter (15 mph max)	lighter than auto (approx. 100 lbs) but heavier than child's scooter	"enough danger" to other vehicles and driver	motor; operator must turn throttle; requires no contact betw. operator & ground; usually "self-propelled"	yes
Byrd (my case)	Segway	12.5 mph max – very close to moped (slower than auto, faster than child's scooter)	105 lbs (very close to moped, much heavier than child's scooter)	analogous to moped – weight and speed pose "enough danger" to driver & other vehicles	motor; operator must lean into direction of travel; if no lean, Segway stops; requires no contact betw. operator & ground; not completely self-propelled	????

[handwritten margin note: doubt?] and the *Monroe* court referenced the *Shipley* reasoning in its statement that the moped "would be able to travel much more quickly than a scooter and is quite a bit heavier than the child's toy...." The reasoning of these two cases taken together suggests that because the Segway is analogous to the moped in terms of speed and weight, the Segway is also analogous to the moped in terms of potential harm.

So far, then, in three of the four relevant categories, the Segway is more analogous to the moped than to the toy scooter. But this does not dictate the result in your situation. Analogical reasoning is not merely a mathematical exercise; it requires you to *weigh* the similarities and differences, not simply to *count* them. You cannot assume that the result in your case will be the same as the result in a previous case just because there are more factual similarities than factual differences. *[handwritten margin note: imp.]* If there is only one factual difference, but that difference relates to a category that was extremely important in the precedential cases, it could outweigh the greater number of similarities.

Here, even though in three of four categories, the Segway seems more analogous to the moped, you must go on to examine that fourth category closely, so that you can determine the relative weight of the facts in that category. Your careful pre-writing up to this point has revealed that the final category — "how normally operated" — was the driving force in the reasoning of both *Shipley* and *Monroe*. Thus, no matter how much the Segway might look and "feel" more like a moped than a scooter, your analysis is not complete until you consider carefully how the Segway i2 SE is normally operated. If its normal operation is more like that of a moped, *then* you can safely answer your question: Mr. Byrd violated the red-light statute and must pay up. However, if its normal operation is more like that of a child's scooter, you may still be able to convince a court that the Segway is more analogous to a scooter, thereby getting Mr. Byrd off the hook.

This brings you to the final cell in your table: how the Segway is normally operated. Before you write anything in this cell, you may need to revisit the *Shipley* and *Monroe* opinions to make sure that you fully understand the court's reasoning about how the operation of the vehicle affected the outcomes of the cases.◗

> ◗ Note that even though you've already read these cases closely and actively (perhaps several times), you may need to read them yet again in the analysis stage. It may not be until this moment that you truly appreciate how important the court's exact words are in enabling you to construct accurate, logical analogies. Do not let this discourage you; even the most experienced lawyers ordinarily read the key portions of important cases multiple times, to make sure they understand them fully.

The *Shipley* court did not explicitly rely upon how the child's scooter was operated in reaching its decision. The outcome in *Shipley appears* to rest solely on speed and weight; the court stated: "[T]he defendant's two-wheeled scooter was too light and too slow to have presented a danger to vehicular traffic traveling through the intersection in the direction of the green light." However, in the very next sentence of its reasoning, the court *implied* that speed was related to how the scooter was normally operated: "The scooter can move only when pushed by one leg of the operator; thus, it is too slow to be an impediment to crossing vehicular traffic."

The reasoning in *Monroe* is more straightforward in its reliance on how the vehicle is normally operated: "While the presence of the motor alone is not dispositive, surely the legislature intended that a vehicle which could be ridden without any contact with the ground and which was usually self-propelled presented enough danger to crossing traffic and to the driver himself to be subject to the vehicular traffic laws."

This review of the court's reasoning suggests that within the category of "how normally operated" there are several important subcategories: whether the vehicle is motorized (although you know this is not dispositive); whether the operator must make contact with the ground; what bodily effort, if any, the operator must make; and whether the vehicle is "usually self-propelled." So your analysis of the Segway's operation requires you to consider whether the Segway is more analogous to a moped or a to child's scooter in each of these subcategories.⬥

> ⬥ Now you can see why it is so important to thoroughly investigate your facts as they relate to all of the relevant categories. You simply cannot go forward with your analysis of the Segway if you have not yet learned the details of its operation.

First, you know the Segway is motorized. Second, you know from your investigation that the operation of the Segway requires no contact between the operator and the ground. Third, you know that to make the Segway go forward, the operator must lean into the direction of travel and that when the operator does not lean forward, the Segway stops. But is the Segway "usually self-propelled"? The answer to this last question is not so obvious, but it may well turn out to be the deciding factor in your analysis.

So how would you go about answering this question? Perhaps you would begin by going all the way back to the automobile and visualizing why its operation makes it "self-propelled." Although the driver must press the gas pedal, this requires only minimal effort; the majority of the automobile's movement is a function of the motor and other physical and mechanical aspects of the vehicle. If the driver lets up on the gas pedal, the automobile will continue its forward motion for a good while.

Next, you would turn to the moped and visualize why its operation makes it "usually self-propelled." The moped driver must twist the throttle lever, but this requires only minimal effort; the majority of the moped's movement is a function of the motor and other physical and mechanical aspects of the vehicle. If the driver loosens the throttle, the moped, like the automobile, will continue its forward motion for a good while.

Then you would turn to the child's scooter and visualize why its operation makes it "not self-propelled." Operating a scooter requires much more than minimal effort from the operator; he must push off from the ground with his leg in a continuous repetitive motion, and his whole body must be engaged to propel the scooter. If he stops pushing off, the scooter will stop almost immediately.

Finally, you would turn to the Segway and visualize its operation. It is motorized, and the operator need not make contact with the ground to make the Segway go. However, the motor will remain engaged only if the operator leans with his full body in the direction of travel. If the operator quits leaning, the Segway will stop cold. Thus, the Segway is not *completely* self-propelled in the same way as the automobile or the moped because of the physical effort required of the operator.

Having thought through the Segway's operation and entered the information into the "how normally operated" column of your table, your analysis is nearly complete. You are now ready to decide whether the Segway is more analogous to the moped or to the child's scooter.

The more reasonable conclusion appears to be that the Segway is more analogous to the moped than to the child's scooter. You have already observed that in three of the four relevant categories (speed, weight, and potential harm to operator and others), the Segway is much more similar to the moped than to the scooter. Further, in the fourth category, "how normally operated," the Segway is somewhat analogous to the moped because it is operated without any contact between the driver and the ground and requires much less effort from the operator than the child's scooter, which requires the operator to constantly push off from the ground. It is true that the Segway is not completely self-propelled; the operator must lean to engage the motor. But this one similarity to the child's scooter likely does not outweigh the cumulative weight of the similarities to the moped.●

> ● Remember: Analogical reasoning is not about *counting* similarities and differences; it is about *weighing* them.

Therefore, taking the information in all four categories together, you could complete your analysis by concluding that the Segway is more analogous to the moped than the toy scooter. And because the controlling case from your jurisdiction, *Monroe*, clearly holds that a moped is "a vehicle such as an automobile" and therefore is subject to the red-light statute, you should advise Attorney Cox that the Segway will likely be considered "a vehicle such as an automobile" as well. Thus, the charges against Mr. Byrd will likely "stick."

8.3 Counteranalysis

Even when your analysis seems to point pretty clearly toward a particular answer, you should not make a final prediction until you force yourself to look at the question from the other direction. In the Segway example, you should be thinking: "Even though the Segway seems an awful lot like a moped, what facts could I use to argue that it's more analogous to a toy scooter?" Put another way, you must always consider whether there is a valid counteranalysis.

The term "counteranalysis" refers to the factual and legal reasoning that would support the result that you have concluded is less likely. It is important to understand that the term "counteranalysis" does not automatically refer to "the other side's argument." In Mr. Byrd's case, for example, your analysis—that the Segway is more analogous to a moped—actually supports the State's position that Mr. Byrd violated the red-light statute.

Thus, you should consider whether there is a valid counteranalysis that would support the conclusion that the Segway is more analogous to a child's scooter and is therefore not "a vehicle such as an automobile." To decide whether this result has any basis in law or fact, you should return to your table and examine it again, this time looking for information that would support the analogy to a child's scooter. Because the information in the first three categories (speed, weight, and potential harm to operator and others) does not support analogizing the Segway to the scooter, the counteranalysis must rest on the information in the "how normally operated" category. Is there anything in that cell that would support the conclusion that the Segway's normal operation is more analogous to the scooter's normal operation than to the moped's normal operation?

The answer has to be "yes." Both the scooter and the Segway require constant bodily effort from the operator to move at all. Just as the toy scooter stops cold when the operator stops pushing off from the ground, the Segway stops cold when the operator stops leaning. Thus, unlike the moped, the Segway is not self-propelled. Even though the Segway is unlike the scooter in terms of speed, weight, and potential harm to the operator and others, it is like the scooter in the one category that was most important to the *Monroe* court's decision.

Thus, the counteranalysis leads to a *valid* result, even though you may legitimately think it is a *weaker* result than the one you reached in your main analysis. Ultimately, in any case, your commission requires you to tell your supervising attorney what the competing outcomes are and why your analysis led you to conclude that the outcome you predicted is more likely than the outcome reached through counteranalysis. If you fulfill this commission, your supervising attorney will be able to make a fully informed decision about how to proceed with the case.

Now, and only now, you are ready to complete the table you've been working on through much of your pre-writing process. Until now, the only possible entry in the "vehicle such as auto? yes or no" column for Mr. Byrd's Segway was "????". You simply could not complete that cell until you completed your analysis. Now, you can replace that "????" with your prediction. Go ahead and write a one-sentence answer to your question: "Yes, Segway is 'vehicle such as auto.'" Then, to remind yourself of the key reasons for your prediction, highlight the information in the Segway row that supports your conclusion. (Note: Whatever you don't highlight would be the basis for the counteranalysis.) Figure 8-4 on the next page is one possible version of the completed table.

The Segway scenario, while it demonstrates a classic analysis using analogical reasoning, also demonstrates why legal analysis can be so frustrating to beginning law students: there are two valid answers to the question of whether the Segway is "a vehicle such as an automobile." While one answer seems stronger, you must recognize that on any given day, either answer *could* persuade the judge and win the day.

Students are often uncomfortable with this reality; they want to know the "right" answer. The instinctive desire to find the "right" answer is normal, but it is not consistent with how the law works. The

Figure 8-4 Completed Table of Segway Analysis

	type of vehicle	speed	weight	potential harm to operator and others	how normally operated	"vehicle such as auto"? yes or no
16 Gra. Gen. Stat. § 2345 (2016).	automobile	fast	very heavy	great potential for danger	motor & operator pressing gas pedal (self-propelled)	yes
Shipley, 872 S.E.2d 278 (Gra. Ct. App. 2017).	child's toy scooter	much slower than auto	much lighter than auto – can be lifted by child	"no danger" to other vehicles	no motor; can move "only if pushed" repetitively by one leg of operator (not self-propelled)	no
Monroe, 872 S.E.2d 425 (Gra. Ct. App. 2017).	moped	slower than auto but faster than child's scooter (15 mph max)	lighter than auto (approx. 100 lbs) but heavier than child's scooter	"enough danger" to other vehicles and driver	motor; operator must turn throttle; requires no contact betw. operator & ground; usually "self-propelled"	yes
Byrd (my case)	Segway	12.5 mph max – very close to moped (slower than auto, faster than child's scooter)	105 lbs (very close to moped, much heavier than child's scooter)	analogous to moped – weight and speed pose "enough danger" to driver & other vehicles	motor; operator must lean into direction of travel; if no lean, Segway stops; requires no contact betw. operator & ground; not completely self-propelled	yes, Segway is "vehicle such as auto" (the charges against Mr. Byrd will stick)

law is inherently ambiguous, and there will often be more than one reasonable answer to a legal question. Once you embrace the reality that there is not always a "right answer" to a legal question, you may discover that legal analysis is more creative, more intellectually challenging, and more fun than you ever thought it could be.

Chapter 8 Recap

What written product(s) do you now have to assist you as you go forward in your pre-writing process?

Segway scenario:
- Bulleted list of aspects of the story that seem important and the questions the story raises in your mind.
- Completed template summarizing parameters of specific assignment(s).
- Tentative research plan.
- Record of research results.
- Detailed notes about each authority, either written on the printed version of the authority or compiled in a separate document.
- *Completed visual representation of analogical categories, including detailed description of relevant similarities and differences between precedential cases and your case.*
- *Prediction of likely answer to your narrow issue.*

Washing machine scenario:
- Bulleted list of aspects of the story that seem important and the questions the story raises in your mind.
- Timeline of key events.
- Completed template summarizing parameters of specific assignment(s).
- Tentative research plan.
- Record of research results.
- Detailed notes about each authority, either written on the printed version of the authority or compiled in a separate document.
- *Completed visual representation of categories, including rule-based result.*
- *Prediction of likely answer to your narrow issue.*

Where are you in terms of issue formulation?

Segway scenario:
- Broad question: Can the charge against Mr. Byrd stick (did he violate the red-light statute)?
- Preliminary narrow issue: Was the Segway he was riding "a vehicle such as an automobile"?
- Note: I didn't find any Segway cases; the cases address two other "vehicles" (toy scooter and moped) that I will need to compare to the Segway.
- Narrower issue: Do the characteristics of a Segway, including its speed, weight, and potential for harm, make it "a vehicle such as an automobile" under the red-light statute? (Need to figure

out how the Segway is like or unlike the toy scooter and the moped discussed in the cases.)

- Even narrower issue: Do the characteristics of a Segway make it "a vehicle such as an automobile" under the red-light statute in light of the relevant categories (speed, weight, potential harm), or normal method of operation (motor? "usually self-propelled"? contact between operator and ground? bodily effort from operator?)?
- *Likely answer to narrow issue: Yes (more analogous to moped than toy scooter).*
- *Likely answer to broad question: Yes, the charge against Mr. Byrd will stick.*

Washing machine scenario:
- Broad question: Does Major Appliances, Inc. have to honor the extended warranty (give Ms. Ward new washer or $)?
- Preliminary narrow issue: How does the timing of events affect the outcome?
- Note: To answer the preliminary narrow issue, I will need to look at both common law and the U.C.C.
- Narrower issue: Does Ms. Ward's timely mailing of her warranty claim to Major Appliances, Inc. preclude Major Appliances, Inc. from denying the claim by alleging that it was never received?
- Still narrower issue: Did Ms. Ward complete the necessary steps to raise the presumption of receipt of notice of warranty claim by Major Appliances, Inc. (properly address envelope, affix proper postage, deposit in mail "in ordinary course" of business)?
- *Likely answer to narrow issue: Yes, she put properly addressed & posted notice in mail in ordinary course of business, so presumption arose that Major Appliances, Inc. received notice.*
- *Likely answer to broad question: Yes, Major Appliances, Inc. must either give Ms. Ward a new machine or give her the money to buy one.*

Independent Practice Exercise 8-1

In Chapter 8, you learned more about how to analyze a legal problem. Using the analytical approach described, decide how Dr. McMahon's question will likely be resolved. This should include completing the visual you constructed in Independent Practice Exercise 7-1 and determining whether there is a valid counteranalysis.

Independent Practice Exercise 8-2

In Chapter 8, you learned more about how to analyze a legal problem. Using the analytical approach described, decide how Mr. Clark's question will likely be resolved. This should include completing the visual you constructed in Independent Practice Exercise 7-2 and determining whether there is a valid counteranalysis.

Independent Practice Exercise 8-3

In Chapter 8, you learned more about how to analyze a legal problem. Using the analytical approach described, decide how Mr. Mordino's question will likely be resolved. This should include completing the visual you constructed in Independent Practice Exercise 7-3 and determining whether there is a valid counteranalysis.

Independent Practice Exercise 8-4

In Chapter 8, you learned more about how to analyze a legal problem. Using the analytical approach described, decide how Mr. Khan's question will likely be resolved. This should include completing the visual you constructed in Independent Practice Exercise 7-4 and determining whether there is a valid counteranalysis.

Chapter 9

Moving from Pre-Writing to Writing

Once you have completed the *pre-writing* process, and only then, you can turn your attention to the *writing* process—the process of formally communicating the results of your work to your reader.

Generally speaking, the steps in the writing process include outlining, drafting, revising, editing, and polishing. If you've done a thorough job in your pre-writing process, you should find that you can move through the outlining and drafting steps of the writing process efficiently and confidently, because you can focus on how to express your analysis rather than on what the analysis should be. In contrast, if you've done no pre-writing, or if you've hurried through your pre-writing process, your analysis will lack depth and creativity, and you will be unable to produce a useful outline, much less a convincing draft.

Without adequate pre-writing, the writing process is extremely frustrating for many law students. Beginning legal writers tend to want their professors to give them examples of finished legal memos that they can use as templates for writing their own memos. In other words, they want to use a "fill-in-the-blank" approach, where they can plug information from their problem into a formula and be done. This is in part because they have achieved great academic success in the past by figuring out what their teachers are looking for and then producing it.⚪

⚪ This is not meant as a criticism; there are times when this strategy is perfectly reasonable and effective. But legal analysis and writing cannot be done well using this strategy.

But legal writing is not that simple. While there are certain organizational structures that most legal writers use effectively (and that most legal readers expect to see), you simply cannot use those *structures* effectively unless you fully understand the *substance* of the particular analysis you are seeking to communicate. This is why careful, thorough pre-writing is necessary and invaluable.

For example, many legal writing textbooks suggest using the "under-does-when" structure for organizing and drafting the issue statement in an objective memo. The "under" refers to the governing rule; the "does" refers to the narrow issue that must be analyzed to answer the broad question;[1] and the "when" refers to the facts of your situation that are most important in resolving the narrow issue. If you have been thorough in your pre-writing process, you will have already identified the governing rule, the narrow issue, and the most relevant facts; so drafting your issue statement is simply a matter of arranging that information using the "under-does-when" structure.

The same principle applies to other parts of legal memos and briefs. There are preferred organizational structures for articulating the governing rules; for explaining the facts, holding, and reasoning of the authorities; for describing the various analogies between your facts and the facts of the authorities; for explaining counteranalysis; and so on. Most legal writing texts suggest using some variation of the IRAC structure (Issue, Rule, Application, Conclusion). Regardless of what structure is suggested, your thorough work at each stage of the pre-writing process will have paved the way for effectively using that structure to convey the information you've identified as necessary to support your analysis.

When you are ready to begin the writing process, you should review your notes on your commission (see Chapter 3). Those notes should contain details about the specific kind of document you are now beginning to write and may also contain information about such aspects of the assignment as format and length. For example, Chapter 3 references three different assignments in connection with the Segway scenario, each of which requires a different kind of written product: an e-mail to Attorney Cox, a formal memo to the file, and a trial brief. Having completed your pre-writing process, you have all the substantive information you need to produce all three of these documents. Your notes on your commission will help you determine such aspects of the written products as tone, length, and format.

Remember that the writing process is recursive rather than linear, meaning that even as you are writing, you may find it necessary to return to some aspect of the pre-writing process to verify information, to find additional authorities, to refine some aspect of your analysis, or in very rare cases, to reconsider your predicted outcome. However, as you become more skilled in moving through the pre-writing process,

---

1. Elsewhere in the memo, you will answer the broad question (perhaps as part of the Brief Answer, or at the outset of the Discussion, or in the Conclusion). But your issue statement should focus the reader on the narrow issues that you will be analyzing in order to arrive at the answer to the broad question.

you will gain confidence in your decision-making, and it will be less likely that you'll have to interrupt your *writing* process to reconsider your *analytical* process.

This book does not cover the writing process itself, nor does it cover legal writing style. Most likely, your legal writing professor has selected one or more of the many available legal writing textbooks for you to use as you learn the structure and style of various kinds of legal documents. Legal writing presents some new challenges for most beginning law students, because it requires absolute precision, clarity, and conciseness. Writing techniques that may have been your strengths as an undergraduate writer (creative word choice, varied sentence structure, etc.) are not highly valued by legal readers.

Working through each pre-writing stage thoroughly and methodically on each legal writing assignment will ease your transition into legal writing. Good pre-writing allows you to determine the content of your analysis *before* you write about it instead of *while* you are writing about it. This logical approach will go a long way toward eliminating your frustration and increasing your satisfaction as you develop into a competent legal writer.

Index